ON THE TURNPIKE

"Deeds, like seeds, take their own time to fructify."

-Mahatma Gandhi

ON THE TURNPIKE

INDIAN ECONOMY SINCE 1947
& INDIAN ECONOMIC SERVICE AT 50

TCA SRINIVASA-RAGHAVAN

MINISTRY OF FINANCE
GOVERNMENT OF INDIA

ACADEMIC FOUNDATION
NEW DELHI

COVER PHOTOGRAPH: Close-up of the dome at the
North Block, New Delhi—office of the Ministry of Finance,
Government of India (Photograph © Anil Ahuja).

DISCLAIMER: While every reasonable effort has been made
to ensure the accuracy of the information contained in this
publication, Ministry of Finance, Government of India and the
publisher accept no liability for errors or omissions. Further,
the findings / views / opinions expressed in this volume are
those of the respective author(s) and do not necessarily reflect
Government's view on the subject.

First published in 2012
by

ACADEMIC FOUNDATION

4772-73 / 23 Bharat Ram Road, (23 Ansari Road),
Darya Ganj, New Delhi - 110 002 (India).
Phones : +91-11-23245001 / 02 / 03 / 04.
Fax : +91-11-23245005.
E-mail : books@academicfoundation.com
www. academicfoundation.com

Cataloging in Publication Data--DK
  Courtesy: D.K. Agencies (P) Ltd. <docinfo@dkagencies.com>

Srinivasa-Raghavan, T. C. A.
  On the turnpike : Indian economy since 1947 & Indian
  economic service at 50 / T.C.A. Srinivasa-Raghavan.
     p.   cm.
  Includes index.
  ISBN 9788171889303

   1. India--Economic conditions--1947- 2. India--Economic
policy--1947- I. Title.

DDC 338.40954   23

Book design and layout: Puja Ahuja and Anil Ahuja.
Printed and bound in India.

10 9 8 7 6 5 4 3 2 1

CONTENTS

Mahatma Gandhi's last steps
at Gandhi Smriti, New Delhi

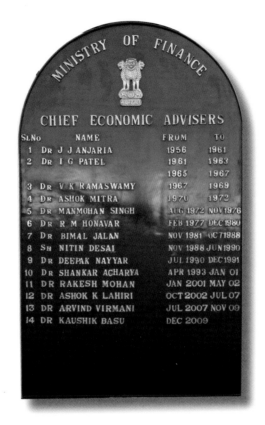

MINISTRY OF FINANCE

CHIEF ECONOMIC ADVISERS

SlNo	NAME	FROM	TO
1	Dr J J ANJARIA	1956	1961
2	Dr I G PATEL	1961	1963
		1965	1967
3	Dr V K RAMASWAMY	1967	1969
4	Dr ASHOK MITRA	1970	1972
5	Dr MANMOHAN SINGH	AUG 1972	NOV 1976
6	Dr R M HONAVAR	FEB 1977	DEC 1980
7	Dr BIMAL JALAN	NOV 1981	OCT 1988
8	Sh NITIN DESAI	NOV 1988	JUN 1990
9	Dr DEEPAK NAYYAR	JUL 1990	DEC 1991
10	Dr SHANKAR ACHARYA	APR 1993	JAN 01
11	DR RAKESH MOHAN	JAN 2001	MAY 02
12	DR ASHOK K LAHIRI	OCT 2002	JUL 07
13	DR ARVIND VIRMANI	JUL 2007	NOV 09
14	DR KAUSHIK BASU	DEC 2009	

ACKNOWLEDGEMENTS:

The original version of the text in this book first appeared in the Business Standard in February 1998. The author wishes to thank the Editor for giving permission to use it as the base material for the narrative in this book.

Grateful thanks to the Editor of the Hindu Business Line, and Mr K Rajendrababu, Chief Librarian of The Hindu Group. Thanks also to the Photo Division, Government of India.

Special thanks to Chitra Narayanan of the Hindu Business Line, to Anil Ahuja who designed the book, to Puja Ahuja for the illustrations, to Bidisha Chaudhuri and Gayatri Nair of the Finance Ministry, to all members of the Indian Economic Service, and of course to the indefatigable Kaushik Basu.

Needless to say, the mistakes are entirely mine.

The plaque above displays the names of Chief Economic Advisers
who have held the office since 1956

FOREWORD

Kaushik Basu

Chief Economic Adviser, Government of India

WHILE the foundations for India's democracy were firmly set at the time of the nation's independence in 1947 and has steadily matured since then, the course of the Indian economy remained uncertain for a long time. Hopes waxed and waned repeatedly over the first three decades. Then from the early 1980s there seemed to be a steady improvement in the pace of growth. This picked up sharply from the early-1990s and then again from 2005, when the economy grew at around 9.5 per cent for three consecutive years. Suddenly India was being described as a major driver of global growth; its corporations were visible in far corners of the world; and its professionals were in demand in India and abroad. Clearly the Indian economy has come a long way from the time of independence. This short book, produced in what is often pejoratively called "coffee table" style, tells the story of this remarkable development trajectory of India and of the Indian Economic Service (IES), created in 1961, to design, shape and manage the economy.

Crafting economic policy is a hazardous job in the best of times. Like the patterns on a zebra, which are at the same time both geometric and arbitrary, economic policy is a strange mixture of the precise and the nebulous. Unlike engineering on the one hand and art on the other, it requires both hard scientific knowledge and intuition and common sense. It is easy for the politician to fall into the trap of believing that there is nothing more to economic policy-making than common sense and to fall into the trap of populism; and it is equally easy for the academic economist to think of economic policymaking as pure science, devoid of the human touch of intuition and judgement.

The engineer entrusted with the task of building an aircraft does not have to deal with this problem. No one argues that the arc of the plane's wing should be decided by majority opinion and the tilt of the aeroplane's nose should be determined by a popular vote. Everybody understands that a plane designed thus would not take off. In fact, that would be the lucky outcome. Yet in economics we have a tendency to equate democracy with populism and rely on the latter. Not surprisingly, many of our economic policies fail to take-off, or descend quickly on doing so.

The truth is that many areas of economics are as professionally demanding as engineering and science. For instance, through years of hard-nosed research we now know how to conduct auctions which make bidders reveal the maximum they are willing to pay, we have hard theorems on different kinds of voting systems and their properties, we have rules on how to respond to a recession by taking fiscal measures, and so on.

What is important is that we use democracy to decide

if we want another plane or a bridge and then use engineers to design the plane or the bridge. Likewise for economics. The direction we take and the broad programmes we adopt should be decided by popular opinion and civil society activism but the design and details of the programmes require professional inputs. In making economic policy this dividing line is not easy to draw; but not to draw it for that reason would be a fatal mistake.

In the case of India, we were lucky that the nation's founding fathers and most notably our first Prime Minister, Jawaharlal Nehru, recognised the importance of professional knowledge in making economic policy. The setting up of the Planning Commission and the Five-Year Plans are all testimony to the Government's recognition of this fact; but the biggest recognition of this came in 1961 in the setting up of the Indian Economic Service. This was a farsighted move, rooted in the recognition that, as the world gets more complex, knowledge and analysis will come to play a more and more dominant role. It was, therefore, essential for an economy aspiring to high targets to have such a service of trained personnel.

As we today celebrate the first fifty years of the IES, there can be no doubt that the importance of this service over the next fifty years will continue to grow. That is the reason why we have been celebrating the Golden Jubilee of the IES by reminding ourselves of the increasing role of knowledge. As part of this celebration we started a new website called Arthapedia.com, which is an open-access

Crafting economic policy is a hazardous job in the best of times. Like the patterns on a zebra, which are at the same time both geometric and arbitrary, economic policy is a strange mixture of the precise and the nebulous.

encyclopedia on the Indian economy that will hopefully evolve as the economy evolves; we produced a calendar, which provides basic information on the Indian economy (a micro-mini economic survey) and celebrates human creativity by displaying twelve portraits of John Maynard Keynes and 11 Nobel economists, all hand-sketched by a leading Indian artist; Oxford University Press is publishing a book of essays on all aspects of the Indian economy written entirely by members of the IES; the Ministry of Finance and the Institute of Economic Growth organised a series of conferences and lectures; and now we have this illustrated book on the history of the IES and the economy.

For writing this we commissioned a distinguished scholar and Senior Associate Editor of The Hindu Business Line, TCA Srinivasa-Raghavan. In keeping with the open traditions of India, we asked him to write this in his own way and to give interpretations to facts and history as he saw fit, without bothering to be "kind to us". On reading the draft, it is evident that he has taken this to heart. Of course, this means that the book comes with the disclaimer that what is written here does not necessarily reflect the views of the Government. What this also means is that while this is not quite the official history of the IES and the Indian economy; it is much more readable for that very reason.

"...there is no alternative but to tread a difficult but determined course. If the opportunities for growth which are so much in evidence are to be seized fully, no effort must be spared in raising resources for the purpose. To flinch from this effort at this stage would be to impose even heavier burdens in the years to come. If we allow the present momentum of growth to wane for the sake of some purely temporary advantage, we will deny ourselves the cumulative benefits of a higher rate of growth for all time to come. If the requirements of growth are urgent, so is the need for some selective measures of social welfare. The fiscal system has also to serve the ends of greater equality of incomes, consumption and wealth, irrespective of any immediate need for resources."

–*Prime Minister Indira Gandhi presenting the Budget for 1970-71*

The then Union Finance Minister Manmohan Singh
holding pre-budget discussions with industrialists
in New Delhi on December 13, 1993.

MESSAGE

Manmohan Singh
Prime Minister of India

I convey this message with great pleasure and a sense of pride. The Indian Economic Service (IES) has completed fifty years. I congratulate all IES officers on the occasion of its Golden Jubilee.

I have been privileged to have worked with the members of the Service on several occasions. I interacted very closely with them as Chief Economic Adviser from 1972 to 1976 and then as Finance Minister from 1991 to 1996. Over the years I have seen the members of IES display professionalism, commitment to duty and intellectual incisiveness. But above all else, they have shown the rare ability of being able to translate abstract intellectual and theoretical ideas into practical policy alternatives.

I understand that the coffee-table book being published to mark the Golden Jubilee celebrations of the IES is not an official history of the service or the Indian economy. But to see what the achievements of the service are we do not really need its history. We only need to look around and see how much India has progressed over the past few decades. Part of the credit for our economic achievements must surely go to the toil and talent of the members of the IES.

I wish the IES the very best in the years to come.

New Delhi
17 January, 2012

MESSAGE

Pranab Mukherjee
Finance Minister of India

The Indian Economic Service (IES) has completed fifty years. The occasion has been commemorated by a number of events and initiatives including a series of lectures, launching of an open-source website called Arthapedia.com that gives economic information in an accessible manner, the release of a calendar featuring hand-sketched portraits of prominent economists, a book of essays by officers of the IES, and, finally, this book authored by a prominent economic journalist.

I congratulate the IES for this initiative and dynamism.

The IES was founded in 1961, at a time when India was attempting to enhance the development process and attain self-reliance. India's first Prime Minister, Pandit Jawaharlal Nehru, had the foresight to realise that for designing and administering economic policy properly a professional cadre of economic professionals dedicated to the task was required. This resulted in the formation of the IES.

The outcome was an institutionalised capacity in the Government to undertake economic analysis for formulating development policy. The aim of the service was to bring economic theory closer to practice. This rationale continues to be the raison d'etre of the IES.

I am fully conscious of the need for professional inputs in the policy-making process and in this role the IES officers excel. I do believe that the need for the service will keep increasing in the decades to come.

I wish the Indian Economic Service a bright and progressive future.

The Finance Minister Pranab Mukherjee delivering the inaugural address at the Roundtable Conference on International Monetary and Financial Systems in New Delhi, on December 17, 1984

THE INDIAN ECONOMIC SERVICE
AN APPRECIATION

'The Task Ahead'

Bimal Jalan
CEA 1982-1992

Why cannot the next generation of IES officers serve at the district level for 5-6 years and give feedback to the officers at the Centre as to what works and what does not work?

"I have spent the longest part of my professional career working very closely with Indian Economic Service Officers. The association began in 1973 when I came to the Ministry of Finance. Thereafter, in the Ministry of Industry as well I worked closely with the Office of the Economic Adviser which was largely manned by IES officers. One could say that I have worked with a whole generation of IES officers.

On this proud occasion of the Golden Jubilee Celebrations of the Service, I would like to felicitate and congratulate the officers and to the younger generation of officers I would like to say to live up to the expectations of the Government.

On this occasion I would like to speak on the role of the Indian Economic Service and Governance. What is it that the Service can do and what would the Service's role be like when the next generation of IES officers meet for their Diamond Jubilee Celebrations.

The emphasis is on what is it that they can contribute towards improvement in governance and policy making. A mix of policies for economic issues like fiscal deficit, inflation control, involves trade offs such as between growth and inflation, growth and equity. This is where policy making becomes crucial.

I would like to focus mainly on two issues where IES officers can play a vital role, which is not being performed at present efficiently. One is the delivery of services like the public distribution system, water availability, provision of electricity, health services, and so on. The other is that why is it that although India has been growing at 8-9 per cent every year, the Human Development Index of the country is among the lowest. It is not that India has had high growth rates only in the recent past, India has been growing at high rates even during the eighties.

What is it that we can do to make use of the talent which has been recruited for the Indian Economic Service?

I would like to pose this challenge to all—why not restructure the Service? At present IES officers are present only at the Centre, but schemes or projects have to be implemented at the state and at the district level. Therefore, the question is how to improve the service delivery at the level of villages and districts. A suggestion is to make the IES a part of the State Service. Like the Indian Administrative Service, why can't we have IES officers at the State level, at least for the next generation of officers?

Earlier, the main concerns were law and order, security

SMALL INDUSTRIES SERVICE INSTITUTE NEW DELHI

Prime Minister Jawahar Lal being explained the working of ghee making machine at the Small Industries Science Institute of the Ministry of Commerce & Industry, New Delhi on April 12, 1958

issues, administration, hence they were given priority. These concerns still remain, but at the same time for delivery of services and governance, it is not the Centre's responsibility. The Centre is responsible for policy making and I am sure IES officers can contribute tremendously in policy mix that is viable.

The issue is why cannot the next generation of IES officers serve at the district level for 5-6 years and give feedback to the officers at the Centre as to what works and what does not work?

Studies need to be taken up on viability of economic issues like PDS, procurement, pricing of grains under the PDS, and so on. Studies on reduction of pilferage and diversion of grains, under the PDS at the ground level also need to be undertaken.

If you look at the empirical data, one finds that the rate of failure in tubewells, rate of diversion in PDS varies across States. Why is it so? There is a need to combine the empirical data with administration to improve implementation.

We have to accept the reality that if you have to make governance effective, then it has to be at the ground level in terms of delivery and at the policy-making level at the Centre. There are trade-offs.

If we bring in the members of the IES at the district and state level, the empirical and research experience can be brought at the ground level to formulate policies which affect the people of India. I think this can make a difference.

The primary message that I want to leave with you is that we should introduce a system to get feedback from the states to improve policy making. It may be a refutable hypothesis but on this occasion we must think how to utilise the best of minds and inputs which the pool of IES officers provide.

We should think of a mechanism whereby the Indian Economic Service can be decentralised.

There is nothing that can stop India from growing at high rates. But the issue is whether this growth contributes to the provision of services which the developed and fastest growing countries provide to their people.

'My IES Colleagues'

Ashok K. Lahiri
CEA, 2002-07

My IES colleagues could always tell me about the relevant data sources, institutional arrangements in any sector, and aspects to be kept in mind in formulating policy in an administratively implementable form.

"I joined the Ministry of Finance in early 1996 as Economic Adviser to the Ministry of Finance. After working at the IMF, and that too on mostly transition economies in Eastern Europe and the former Soviet Union, for almost a decade, this was quite a change. Working conditions were somewhat different. But, there was a lot of excitement from the growth momentum that the Indian economy had achieved, post-reforms, after the balance of payments crisis in 1990-91. This excitement, along with the colleagues that I got to work with, more than made up for the differences in working conditions.

The colleagues in the Economic Division were mostly IES officers. They belonged to the IES cadre, which was constituted in 1961 to build the capacity of the Government for tackling the issues of development and poverty reduction by rendering suitable economic advice and playing an active role in economic administration. What amazed me was the ready availability of some IES colleagues who could always tell me about the relevant data sources, institutional arrangements in any sector, and aspects to be kept in mind in formulating policy in an administratively implementable form.

After a couple of years at the Ministry, I went on 'foreign assignment' to National Institute of Public Finance and Policy and came back to the Ministry as CEA in 2002. The vulnerability on the balance of payments front had not only virtually disappeared with foreign exchange reserves growing from about $22 billion in 1996 to over $75 billion in 2003, but was getting replaced by the new challenge of how to sterilise inflows of foreign reserves and contain inflation. New concerns had arisen on the fiscal front as well. My responsibilities as CEA were manifold compared to what they were earlier as an Economic Adviser. As CEA, I had the benefit of interacting with IES officers on a very wide field. These interactions broadened my horizons.

Policy decisions pertaining to various sectors of economy required detailed analysis not only of developments taking place in specified sectors but in all sectors and across sectors, as also across countries, so as to maximise the benefits and opportunities that are potentially available in a globalised economy. No matter whether it was edible oil prices or the Fiscal Responsibility and Budget Management Act, the IES cadre had extremely competent officers who could always steer the analysis along – at least what I thought as – the right path."

'A Unique Service'

Nitin Desai
CEA, 1988-90

The IES has permeated every corner of the economic policy apparatus at the Centre... liberalisation and a growing reliance on indirect ways of influencing market outcomes have increased the salience of economics in policy making.

"THE Indian Economic Service was born at a time when the Government of India intervened extensively in the operation of markets and this required sound analysis and advice on the modalities of intervention. The need for this expertise was greatest in the Planning Commission, the Finance Ministry and the Ministry of Commerce and Industry. But soon the other economic ministries also felt the need for economists and the IES permeated every corner of the economic policy apparatus at the Centre.

But the role of the Service is not just a consequence of a dirigiste ideology. In fact liberalisation and a growing reliance on indirect ways of influencing market outcomes have increased the salience of economics in policy making. Even in the earlier days of direct controls the new thinking on issues like cost-benefit analysis and tax policy that found its place in policy was not just a product of the 'outsiders' who were inducted into the Government. It needed the systematic analysis and economic mind-set that was provided by members of the Service

The Indian Economic Service has a unique place in the bureaucratic structure. It is a service that is almost exclusively devoted to policy advice rather than to the implementation of policies in specific cases. This puts the members of the Service in close contact with the political executive. But it also leads to some inter-service rivalry with the Indian Administrative Service, which lays claim to being the first among equals and hence the political executive's policy adviser by right and, to a lesser extent with the Indian Revenue Service which lays claim to economic expertise at least in the crucial area of tax policy.

There was another rather special feature that shapes the IES — the lateral induction of economists who have established their reputation outside the Government. This is often resented by the members who came through the civil service examination. But these 'outsiders' have helped to raise the profile of economists in the highest reaches of policy making and created a certain incentive among the members of the Service to keep in touch with advances in economic thinking and methods.

I had the good fortune of working with members of the IES both in the Planning Commission and in the Finance Ministry and I join all past and present members of the IES in wishing the Service more by way of success and recognition in the years to come."

Finance Minister Madhu Dandavate addressing Chief Executives of Public Sector firms at a meeting in New Delhi on January 30, 1990.

FINANCE SECRETARY

Dr. NITIN DESAI
SECY & CEA

वित्त म...

मुख...

FINANCE A...

EXECU...

Immaculate Conception

On July 26,1952, the Cabinet decided that the Planning Commission should appoint a Committee to examine the question of establishing statistical cadres to serve the general needs of different ministries and, if possible, of different States in the case of important posts. The Committee submitted its report in September, 1953. Here's the story of the formation of IES.

"*It was also decided that the existing staff in the various ministries doing economic and statistical work should be absorbed as far as possible in either of the two services, depending upon their fitness and qualifications. Such as were left over, would continue to work as at present.*"

-Excerpt from the proposal to constitute IES
February 12, 1958

Jawahar Lal Nehru addressing the midnight session of the Constituent Assembly of India

PROPOSAL, DISCUSSION AND OUTCOME

Why the economic and statistical setvice were not combined

On July 26,1952, the Cabinet decided that the Planning Commission should appoint a Committee:—

1) to examine the question of establishing statistical cadres to serve the general needs of different ministries and, if possible, of different states in the case of important posts;

2) to review the existing posts and personnel with a view to redistributing them for a more balanced development of statistical work; and to formulate the future needs of trained personnel.

3) In pursuance of this decision, the Planning Commission appointed a Committee under the chairmanship of Shri VT Krishnamachari

2.   The Committee submitted its report in September, 1953, recommending the formation of a Service to be known as the Statistical and Economic Advisory Service. The report of the Committee contains the following principal conclusions and recommendations:—

1) The present practice of each ministry making its own arrangements with the Union Public Service Commission (UPSC) for recruiting personnel causes inconvenience and delay. Moreover, considerable hardship is caused by keeping almost two-thirds of the entire staff on a temporary basis for an indefinite period. There is, therefore, an immediate need for an integrated Service which would offer the necessary security and assist in developing a unified outlook among the personnel;

2) Opinion in the States is not yet favourable to participation in a common cadre with the Centre but it is likely that as States gradually realise the advantages of the Service there will be requests from them for qualified personnel. While, therefore, the proposed Service may be confined to the Centre initially a few additional posts at supervisory level should be kept in reserve to meet such requests.

3) Senior economists and statisticians with long professional experience who may have to be recruited directly from Universities and other fields on special contracts and ad-hoc scales of pay would hardly fit into a regular Service like the one proposed. Regarding the rest it would appear that for nearly a quarter of the total number of posts a degree in Economics with Statistics is prescribed as an essential qualification. Again, for over one half of the total number, Economics with Statistics is one of the alternative qualifications. It is, therefore, preferable to constitute a single Service called the Statistical and Economic Advisory Service which would be open to graduates with primary qualifications in Statistics or Economics.

4) There are special considerations in the case of the staff in the Ministries of Defence and Railways. The present system in the two ministries may continue but if in future the need arose in either of them for trained economists and statistician from outside then it should be met from the Cadre;

COPY NO. 41

MEETING OF THE CABINET HELD ON WEDNESDAY, THE 12TH FEBRUARY, 1958, AT 4.45 PM

Case No .44/9/58

PROPOSAL TO CONSTITUTE A STATISTICAL AND ECONOMIC SERVICE/A STATISTICAL SERVICE

PRESENT

Shri Jawarharlal Nehru, Prime Minister.

Maulana Abul Kalam Azad, Minister of Education and Scientific Research.

Shri Govind Ballabh Pant, Minister of Home Affairs.

Shri Jagjivan Ram, Minister of Railways.

Shri Gulzarilal Nanda, Minister of Labour & Employment and Planning.

Shri T.T Krishnamachari, Minister of Finance.

Shri Lal Bahadur Shastri, Minister of Transport and Communications.

Sardar Swaran Singh, Minister of Steel, Mines & Fuel.

Shri K.C Reddy, Minister of Works, Housing and Supply.

Shri Ajit Prasad Jain, Minister of Food & Agriculture.

Shri V.K Krishna Menon, Minister of Defence.

Shri S.K Patil, Minister of Irrigation & Power.

ALSO PRESENT

Shri V.T.Krishnamachari,Deputy Chairman, Planning Commission.

Shri Asoke Kumar Sen, Minister of Law.

Professor P.C Mahalanobis, Honorary Statistical Adviser to Cabinet.

SECRETARIAT

Shri N.R Pillai.

Shri P.A Gopalakrishnan.

The Cabinet decided that two separate Services should be formed; one a Statistical Service and other an Economic Service.With regard to the Statistical Service, all the proposals of the Home Ministry contained in para 11.3 of the summary were approved. It was also decided that the existing staff in the various ministries doing economic and statistical work should be absorbed as far as possible in either of the two Services, depending upon their fitness and qualifications. Such as were left over, would continue to work as at present.

2. It was further decided that control of the two Services should vest in the Ministry of Home Affairs. For working out detailed schemes for the constitution of the two Services, a Committee was set up, consisting of Cabinet Secretary as the Chairman and the Honorary Statistical Adviser and representatives of the Home Ministry and other ministries concerned and the Planning Commission, as members.

5) There should be six grades in the Statistical and Economic Advisory Service—

Grade I	Directors	Rs 1300-1800
Grade II	Joint Directors	Rs 1000-1400
Grade III	Deputy Director	Rs 600-1150
Grade IV	Assistant Director	Rs 350-850
Grade V	Senior Investigator	Rs 275-500
Grade VI	Junior Investigator	Rs 160-450

The permanent strength of each grade in the Service will be determined by adding 80 per cent of semi-permanent posts to the existing permanent posts;

6) For fitting the existing personnel into the appropriate grades a Special Selection Board presided over by the Chairman of the UPSC should be constituted including in addition, a member of the UPSC, a senior Economic Adviser to Government, the Statistical Adviser to the Cabinet and a senior officer of the Ministry of Finance.

7) Keeping in view the need for ensuring reasonable prospects of promotion to existing personnel on the one hand and the desirability of providing for absorption at various levels of fresh talent on the other, the following procedure is recommended for the future recruitment:–

- **Junior Investigators:** All vacancies should be thrown open for direct recruitment through competitive examination and/or interview held by the UPSC.

- **Senior Investigators:** All vacancies should be filled by promotion from Junior Investigators on the basis of departmental test and strict seniority in the ratio of 2:1 respectively.

- **Assistant Directors:** 50 per cent of the vacancies should be filled by direct recruitment on the basis of competitive examination and or interview held by the UPSC and 50 per cent by promotion from Senior Investigators.

- **Deputy Directors:** Normally by promotion from Assistant Directors with at least four years service in their grade. Promotion will be based entirely on merit.

- **Joint Directors:** Deputy Directors with at least six years service in their grade would be eligible for promotion as Joint Directors. The promotion will be based entirely on merit. The

Controlling Authority will be free to suggest that a particular vacancy should be filled by direct recruitment from outside.

- **Directors:** The Joint Directors with at least two years service in their grade and at least eight years of total service in the grades of Deputy Directors and Joint Directors will be eligible for promotion as Director. The promotion will be based entirely on merit. The Controlling Authority will be free to suggest that a particular vacancy should be filled by direct recruitment from outside.

8) The Ministry of Home Affairs will be the Controlling Authority for the Service. Postings and transfers of personnel will be made on the advice of a Statistical and Economic Advisory Board to be set up consisting of the Cabinet Secretary as Chairman, and four members of whom two will be Secretaries of participating ministries, one head of a statistical organisation and one Senior Economic Adviser to the Government of India. The Establishment Officer of the Government of India will provide the Secretariat for the Board Officers of the Service, when posted to a particular ministry, will be under the administrative control of that ministry for all purpose and in special requirement of particular ministries will be taken into account.

9) The Controlling Authority should be asked to review the progress of the Service from time to time and suggest such re-organisation of statistical work and redistribution of posts and personnel as may be necessary. In particular, the existing designations of statistical and economic posts are in some cases misleading. The necessary detailed examination should be undertaken in consultation with ministries with a view to ensuring a uniform nomenclature.

10) Soon after the Statistical and Economic Advisory Service is constituted, the Controlling Authority should take an opportunity to consult the State Governments in regard to the probably requirements of qualified staff for their economic and statistical organisations.

11) If the growing need for trained personnel is to be satisfactorily met the existing institutions for advanced professional training should be strengthened.

3.   The recommendations of the Committee together with its report were circulated to all the ministries for their views. From the comments of the ministries it appeared that they unanimously approved the need and formation of a Statistical and Economic Advisory Service. They, how-

ever, raised certain objections of a minor nature here and there. In fact, even the Ministry of Defence, who, along with the Ministry of Railways, were proposed to be excluded from participating in the Service, on special grounds, came forward with the plea that they should not be prevented from joining the Service in so far as their civilian statistical personnel were concerned. The Ministry of Finance (Department of R. & E.) however, reserved their comments pending the availability of the views of Professor PC Mahalanobis, Honorary Statistical Adviser to the Cabinet.

4. Professor Mahalanobis forwarded his views to the Finance Minister on 1st April, 1956. Therein he lays stress on the statistical work relating to planning and has suggested an alternative scheme for the creation of a "Central Statistical Pool" to cater to the needs of planning. He does not favour the idea of a combined Statistical and Economic Advisory Service on the lines of Administrative Service as he feels that purely economic advisory duties should not be mixed up with technical and professional work in statistics. According to him, the work now being done in offices of Economic Advisers is primarily statistical in nature and officers in charge of such work should properly belong to the Statistical Pool. For the economic side, he feels that the most appropriate way of getting able and up-to-date advice would be to consult outstanding economists individually or in groups or appoint them on contract basis. Prof Mahalanobis maintains that his scheme is not the final one, but it can serve as a basis for discussion. It is designed to serve the needs of the Centre as also the States, universities, scientific and technological institutions and public authorities or enterprises by mutual agreement. Prof Mahalnobis suggests further that the details of the scheme can be worked out by an Ad hoc Committee in consultation with the Cabinet Secretariat, the Planning Commission, the Central Statistical Office, the Finance Ministry, the Home Ministry and the UPSC.

5. The scheme of Prof Mahalanobis was circulated to all the ministries on 15th May, 1956. Comments of the majority of the ministries were received. Some of the ministries are generally in agreement with the idea of a Pool, but have raised certain doubts requiring clarification. The ministries which are critical of Prof Mahalanobis's scheme are the ministries of Food and Agriculture, Commerce & Industry and Iron and Steel.

6. On examining the scheme of a Statistical and Economic Advisory Service as recommended by the Krishnamachari Committee and, a Central Statistical Pool formulated by Prof Mahalanobis, it appeared that there was hardly any meeting ground between the two. The following will reveal some of the basic differences between the two schemes:-

	Statistical & Economic Advisory Service	Central Statistical Pool
1.	It should be a composite Service and should include both statistical and economic advisory posts.	It should consist of only statistical posts.
2.	Minimum and maximum pay should be Rs 160 and Rs 1800.	Minimum and maximum pay should be Rs 275 and Rs 2500 (with two selection grade posts going upto Rs 3000 or whatever may be the top salary of the IAS Cadre).
3.	The Controlling Authority should be the Ministry of Home Affairs assisted by a Board of Officials.	The Controlling Authority should vest in the Cabinet Secretariat. (to be helped by the Central Statistical Organisation in technical matters) and assisted by a Board of officials and non-officials.
4.	It should consist of only regular posts.	There should be two kinds of posts; Group 1—Regular posts Group 2—Assignment posts (to be for short period).

7. It was, therefore, decided that the matter should be referred to the Economic Committee of Secretaries, to which representatives of the Ministry of Home Affairs should be invited, and their views ascertained, before a paper was submitted to the Cabinet for its orders.

8. The Economic Committee of Secretaries, accordingly, discussed the matter on 4th December, 1956, and examined in particular, whether an Economic and Statistical Service, as recommended by the Krishnamachari Committee or a Statistical Pool proposed by Prof Mahalanobis was more suitable to the needs of Government. It was pointed out that in certain ministries like Railways, Food, Agricultural and Labour it was not merely statistics that was wanted but also economic advice. Advice on price fixation and controls, exports and imports of specified agricultural commodities and investigations of an economic character could not be had from men trained only in statistics. Nor was it considered practicable for these ministries to seek ad hoc economic advice from outside economists in respect of these matters.

9. The Committee, therefore, reached the following conclusions:—

   1) An Economic and Statistical Service as recommended by Krishnam-

achari Committee is preferable to the Statistical Pool proposed by Prof Mahalanobis. The Service should include all posts upto and including those of Joint directors in the proposed scale of Rs 1000-50-1400.

2) In addition to the regular service, there should be a pool of economic experts on which the Central and State Governments could draw for their needs if and when necessary.

3) The qualifications for recruitment to the Service should include Economics or Statistics as recommended by the Krishnamachari Committee.

4) There should be provision for direct recruitment to a certain percentage of the posts in each grade.

5) The Controlling Authority should be the Ministry of Home Affairs assisted by a Board of officials, as suggested in para 10 of Annexure 3 of the Krishnamachari Committee's Report.

10. A note was prepared by the Cabinet Secretariat on the basis of the various views then available, seeking approval of the Cabinet in principle to the constitution of an Economic and Statistical Service on the lines suggested by the Economic Secretaries Committee. The note was forwarded on 18th January, 1957 to the Ministry of Home Affairs/ Finance, and, a copy of it was sent to Prof P. C. Mahalanobis on 31st January, 1957. Subsequently it was also sent to the Planning Commission for their comments.

11. 1. The Ministry of Finance agreed with the broad conclusions in the note but suggested "that while administrative control may be exercised through the Board in the Ministry of Home Affairs, the functional control and direction will have to be assumed by the Department of Economic Affairs. This functional direction and coordination will be achieved by inter-departmental discussions and by close liaison with the Chief Economic Adviser in the Department of Economic Affairs of this Ministry".

11. 2. The Planning Commission are of the view that there should be a combined Statistical and Economic Advisory Service with two wings, one for Statisticians and another for Economists.

11.3. The views of the Ministry of Home Affairs are as follows:-

(i) A separate Statistical Service would be more homogeneous than a combined Statistical and Economic Advisory Service. Statistics has grown into a self-sufficient science. It is mainly concerned with the collection and interpretation of facts and figures but these are not confined solely to economic matters. Statistics cover the entire social field. Economics is no doubt related, to some extent, to and assisted by Statistics. But both are highly specialised and it might create difficulties if Statisticians and Economic Advisers are lumped together into one group.

(ii) At each level in the Service there should be room for filling vacancies by direct recruitment as well as by promotion strictly on the basis of pure merit.

(iii) Recruitment should be made by the U.P.S.C. The normal procedure of recruitment, subject to such exceptions as may be necessary, should govern this Service.

(iv) The Ministry of Home Affairs agree that the scheme for the new Service should provide for an interchange of personnel with the universities and higher scientific institutions. They accordingly support the suggestions that a certain number of permanent posts should be earmarked to be filled by temporary appointments of qualified statisticians from universities and higher scientific institutions, and that Government statisticians should be deputed to work in universities for a prescribed period from time to time. Deputation of Government statisticians to work in universities, etc. for some months, would also be a healthy arrangement. It would enable them to keep abreast of the latest developments in their field; and the universities etc. would benefit by contact with men handling practical work. This would be a characteristic feature of this Service.

(v) Considering the practical context of statistical work, it would be desirable to recruit to this Service young men who, besides possessing special qualifications in Statistics, have wide general education so that they may combine the human with the scientific approach. Perhaps apart from papers in Statistics, candidates appearing for the Statistical Service might also be examined in general subjects prescribed for the competitive examination for recruitment to the superior Services.

(vi) This Ministry would also like the question of these and of other candidates approved for various branches of Central Services to be trained in the Administrative school to be examined.

12.1. The Honorary Statistical Adviser to the Cabinet re-examined the matter carefully and he is of the view that future development of statistical work of Government would be better assisted by constituting a separate Service of Statisticians rather than a combined Statistical and Economic Advisory Service.

In fact, the Cabinet in their decision of 26 July, 1952, had directed that the Committee of the Planning Commission should examine the question of establishing statistical cadres to serve the general needs of ministries, and, if possible, of different States, in the case of important posts. It is his view that the purely economic advisory duties should not be mixed up with technical and professional work in statistics. He has pointed out that arrangements for producing trained statisticians did not exist in India until recently. Before 1943 Elementary Statistics was taught as part of a course in Economics. Naturally, many among the older staff, who are doing statistical work, have been drawn from among economics graduates. The Master's degree in Statistics began to be awarded in India only since 1943 and facilities for post-M Sc professional training in Statistics became available 10 years later in the Central Statistical Organisation, the Indian Statistical Institute and the Indian Council of Agricultural Research. As long as arrangements for producing competent professional statisticians did not exist one had to make good with whatever talent was available. The statistical work in Government offices also used to be done at a fairly elementary level. There were no high stakes involved, requiring correct and comprehensive statistical data and their valid analysis. Much of the work was merely routine compilation of stereotyped returns or was concerned with writing of notes and memoranda for superior officers.

12.2 This type of work continues to be needed and is useful, but this is no substitute for real statistical work which can only be done satisfactorily by competent, professionally trained statisticians. As trained specialists in statistics are now being produced in adequate numbers, it is only proper and reasonable that important statistical posts in Government should be filled only by statisticians of high technical competence. The recommendation of the Committee that a Joint Economic and Statistical Service be created, the qualifications for recruitment being a degree in Economics and/or Statistics, seems to him, to be based on an inadequate appreciation of the degree of specialisation demanded by Economics or Statistics at higher level of posts. It is no longer possible for an economist or a statistician, however, competent in his own field, to do actually well the work of the other. Interchangeability is of the essence of a common Service, and if this is fundamentally absent, the very basis of a common Service does not exist. On this argument, the proposal to have a common Service of Economists and Statisticians, with separate wings for each group, would appear to suffer from the same disadvantage. If the wings are as clearly independent and separate that the only element binding them together is the similarity of scales of pay and conditions of service each wing might as well be described as a separate Service. If it is not so, and a really integrated Service is being considered, the resultant incongruities would perhaps be no less when the common Service is supposed to have two wings, than when it has none. Moreover, modern Statistics is a developed science of very wide and general applica-

tion. Economics is only one of the fields where it finds use. Statisticians would be equally concerned with the application of statistical techniques in agriculture, plant and animal genetics, population, health scientific research, industry, communication, education, personnel selection, and planning etc. etc.

12.3 It is recognised that there would be increasing need for the collection and analysis of reliable statistical data in diverse fields for purposes of planning for the assessment of progress in the implementation of plans, and generally for enabling rational decisions to be taken on many economic, social and administrative problems which come up for the consideration of Government from time to time. Modern advances in Statistics have made it possible to extract much more information at a given cost, and with much greater speed, than was thought possible before. Techniques of sampling have been to carry out surveys which can provide reliable quantitative assessment of social and economic conditions in different parts of a big country at comparatively low costs. In addition to the traditional role of Statistics of furnishing data and methods for economic analysis, modern statistical techniques have innumerable applications in many fields of agriculture, industry, science, technology, education, plant and animal genetics, population etc; and in all these fields, modern statistical methods are in a position to make a significant contribution. The development of statistical theory and its application to practical problems has been accompanied by spectacular developments in the methods and equipment for data processing; the advent of electronic computers has indeed brought about a virtual revolution in technical methods and opened the possibility of a very complex analysis of data being undertaken and completed within a short time.

12.4 These extremely useful and efficient techniques of collection, processing, analysis and presentation of data require highly specialised knowledge of statistical theory and professional training and experience of applying modern statistical methods to practical problems. A proper organisation for statistical work, which may be expected to meet the requirements of a modern state working for a socialist order of society, would have to be staffed with fully qualified professional statisticians, trained and experienced in professional statistical work in different fields.

12.5 In order to attract good talent to statistical offices of the Government, provide this specialised staff with security of tenure and prospects or advance in their own line, and to develop among them a unified outlook imbued with scientific objectivity, a separate cadre for statisticians is considered necessary. The need for the establishment of a cadre of statisticians also arises from the fact that the present practice of each ministry making its own arrangement with the UPSC for recruitment of personnel in its statistical office causes inconvenience and much delay, and hampers proper utilisation of available technical manpower. As a large proportion of those who apply for such technical posts come from some Government office or other, it is clear that a more flexible and rational use of statistical personnel would be possible if there is a separate integrated Service of statisticians.

13.1   In Prof Mahalanobis's view, therefore, it would be undesirable and incongruous to have a combined Statistical and Economic Advisory Service. He has advised that a Service for trained statisticians should be created and that it should be kept distinct from any cadre of Economists, which might be separately formed if considered necessary. The suggestion of a separate Service for Statisticians does not in any way imply that the Economists and Statisticians would work in isolation from each other, or one or the other group is less or more important. It is necessary that a Statistician, handling economic data, should have sound background of Economics just as it would be desirable for an Economist dealing with quantitative data to have good appreciation of statistical tools and techniques. A primarily Economic Advisory Section may have Statisticians (belonging to the Statistical Cadre) in its staff and Statistical Offices may have economic analysts when required. The establishment of a separate cadre of Statisticians does not come in the way of closer functional integration of work of the Statisticians and Economists. The Economist will have to rely for his facts on the Statistician, and the Statistician should serve various real needs, which of course include the need of proper economic interpretation of a given situation.

13.   2. The other points made by him are:-

(i)   The Statistical Service or Pool should be organised as a Scientific Service (as distinguished from Administrative Services). The structure of Scientific Services in the Council of Scientific & Industrial Research can be generally adopted with suitable modifications.

(ii)   A suitable portion of vacancies (say, 50 or 60 percent) should be filled by promotion which should be made by a Selection Board on the basis of competitive examinations and/or evaluation of technical ability by competent statisticians.

(iii)   There would also be provision for direct recruitment at all levels to maintain a high quality of professional work.

(iv)   There should be provision for qualified statisticians from Universities and higher scientific institutions to work on special projects in temporary Government posts and a number of permanent posts should be reserved for such tem-

porary appointments. Selected Government statisticians should also be sent from time to time to work in universities and higher scientific institutions for several months or a year.

(v)   Among the present statistical staff those who have acquired competence in technical work in Statistics should be absorbed in the new Service, the selection should be made on the basis of technical qualifications as assessed by statisticians.

(vi)   It is neither necessary for desirable to include all existing officers in the new Service. Those who are not included need not necessarily be thrown out, but may continue in the grades to which they were originally appointed; and thus would have the opportunity of applying (and getting selected if they are found suitable) for Service vacancies.

14.   Summing up, it will be seen that while the Ministry of Home Affairs and the Honorary Statistical Adviser to the Cabinet (Prof PC Mahalanobis) are of the view that a separate Statistical Service is desirable, the Committee of Economic Secretaries, the Ministry of Finance and some other ministries including Food and Agriculture, Labour, Commerce and Industry and Defence, which have large statistical cadres have expressed preference for a combined Statistical and Economic Service. In the opinion of the Planning Commission there should be a combined Statistical and Economic Service with two separate wings, one for Economists and one for Statisticians.

15.   1. Orders of the Cabinet are now solicited on the following points:-

(1)   Whether a combined Economic and Statistical Service should be constituted, as recommended by the Krishnamachari Committee or whether a separate Statistical Service should be formed, as proposed by the Honorary Statistical Adviser and agreed to by the Ministry of Home Affairs.

(2)   If a combined Economic and Statistical Service is approved, whether it should have (a) a Statistical Wing and Economic Wing, as recommended by the Planning Commission and (b) whether it should integrate the features recommended by the Economic Committee of Secretaries (vide para 9.1 to 4).

(3)   Whether the Controlling Authority for the combined Economic and Statistical Service should be the Ministry of Home Affairs, assisted by a Board of officials as suggested

by the Economic Committee of Secretaries, or whether functional control and direction should vest in the Ministry of Finance (Department of Economic Affairs) leaving only administrative control to be exercised through the Board in the Ministry of Home Affairs.

The Cabinet Secretariat is of the view that control, whether administrative or financial, should vest only in one ministry and the appropriate ministry for the purpose is the Ministry of Home Affairs.

(4) If the formation of a separate Statistical Service is approved, whether it should integrate the following features:-

(a) Division of the Service into certain specified grades

(b) Provision of a specified percentage of posts in each grade to be filled up by direct recruitment;

(c) Provision of a number of permanent posts in the higher grades to be earmarked for being filled up by temporary appointments of qualified statisticians from universities, higher scientific institutions and if available, from

the other Government services and

(d) Provision for deputation of Government Statisticians to work in universities etc.

(e) Control of the Service to vest in the Ministry of Home Affairs.

15.2. After orders are passed on the above points, a detailed scheme will be drawn up by the Ministry of Home Affairs, providing for method of recruitment, educational qualifications required, age of entry and grades of pay with categories of posts etc. to be included in the Service and submitted to the Cabinet for its approval before it is implemented.

15.3. This note has been seen by the Honorary Statistical Adviser and the Ministry of Home Affairs and approved by the Prime Minister.

Sd/-
(P.A. Gopalakrishnan)
Joint Secretary to the Cabinet.
Dated the 17th January,1958

The Age of Innocence

(1947-1957)

It was the era of fiscal rectitude, of striving for balanced budgets, and of not squeezing the middle-class on the grounds of sacrifice for future generations.

F EW jobs are more exacting than what India's finance ministry does. On the one hand, it has to ensure the continuing good health of public finances; on the other, there are the pulls and pressures of a genuine pluralist democracy. Reconciling the two objectives, as the experience of independent India shows, is a Sisyphian task. Just when a Finance Minister thinks he's got there, the rock rolls right down again. Rising expenditure and falling revenues are staple diet to all finance ministers, not just in India but the world over.

The first man to whom the task of managing the independent India's fisc fell was RK Shanmukham Chetty, a businessman from Madras with no particular expertise in the business of running government finances. He presented the first Budget of independent India on November 26, 1947. It was an interim one, as it covered only seven and a half months of the year. India had just been partitioned, which meant a huge fiscal load from paying off Pakistan and paying for the refugees as a result of the Partition. The world had just come out of the biggest war ever so that the world economy was in shambles, and because of demobilisation, the defence services were gobbling up the bulk of the Government's revenues. In those days, defence expenditure got mentioned ahead of 'civil estimates'. Chetty said the difficulties that faced the country and the Government's efforts to bridge the gap between expenditure and revenue simply would not go away.

Perhaps the most important part of Chetty's speech was the reference to high levels of taxation and cheap borrowing by the Government. He said that the Central Board of Directors of the Reserve Bank of India (RBI) had admonished the Government for this. Both were proving a disincentive for private industry. Chetty's response was conciliatory. But he was able to keep only half his promises. While he didn't raise taxes, he did leave the deficit—Rs 25 crore—uncovered, thus deciding to persist with the policy

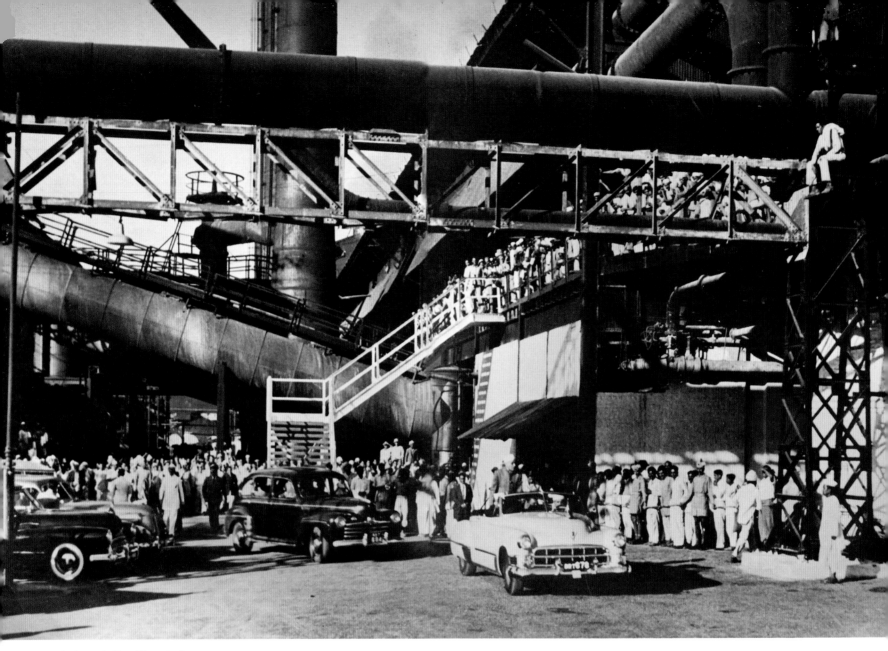

A view of a Tata Plant: India
begins to industrialise

of cheap government borrowing on the grounds that it was necessary in the national interest. Another legacy that Shanmukham Chetty left behind was a restrictive import policy. "The rapid depletion of sterling balances is causing some anxiety to the Government," he said and proceeded to divide imports into three categories: free, restricted and prohibited. Over the years the first category almost vanished while the latter two continued to grow. Thus was born import licensing.

In the next Budget for 1948-49 Chetty started another practice—of raiding the railways surplus. He reduced taxes with two objectives: to increase the rate of savings which was a paltry 4 per cent of GDP and to increase private investment. He was thus the original Laffer Curver practitioner. But the rate of savings didn't pick up, nor did private investment.

Sometime in 1948, Chetty was removed by Nehru for something which, even in those days, was considered a very minor misdemeanour. Indeed, he was removed on a mere suspicion. His place was taken by John Mathai who, in his maiden Budget speech, articulated the two problems that dogged India: inflation and chronic forex shortage. Prices, said Mathai, are rising and hard currency reserves are dwin-

Jawahar Lal Nehru at the foundation laying ceremony of the Indian Statistical Institute.

(Top right) A view of the proceedings during a two-day conference of chief ministers and finance ministers, presided over by Union Finance Minister Chintaman Deshmukh in New Delhi on October 14, 1952.

dling when it should be the other way round. This was the third time in a row that a finance minister had rung the alarm and if the same statements had been made five years later—as indeed they were—they would have been followed by a string of restrictive measures and controls. But the air had not thickened yet and the approach was one of economic liberalism. There wasn't the slightest hint of the detailed controls that were to follow in less than a decade. True, the economy was small and rudimentary and there was only so much that a Finance Minister could do. Still, it is impossible not to be struck by the general refrain which is one of economic liberalism.

THE next two years were unremarkable in the fiscal sense but they did leave behind two legacies: the Planning Commission—over the setting up of which Mathai resigned—and the Estimates Committee, which the new Constitution required. Indeed, the second of John Mathai's budgets was remarkable only for the discussion it contained of the new requirements placed on it by the Constitution. Sadly, the speeches imparted no special flavour of the new administrative and political problems which resulted from the new Constitution. The finance ministry had been given a new

course to steer and it was up to it how it would do it.

Late in 1950 Mathai quit and was replaced by a former ICS officer, Chintaman Deshmukh. He would run the Finance Ministry for the next six years, presenting six budgets in a row. He was lucky to manage the economy during a rare and prolonged good period. He suffered, in the words of a contemporary, "the consequences of good fortune." Unlike the previous four years, his tenure saw reversal in inflation. Prices began to fall as world commodity prices plummeted and India began to import large volumes (partly, as John Mathai had been candid enough to admit, in order to realise some much needed customs revenue). Industrial production grew at a healthy rate of 4 cent and agriculture also picked up. The obverse side to this was slow export growth and a continuing dip in forex reserves about which, at least according to BK Nehru who was by then in charge of India's external finances, no one seemed to care much about. The Commerce Minister, TT Krishnamachari, was an import-hawk and had convinced the Prime Minister Jawahar Lal Nehru that quick growth could be achieved by large-scale imports.

These were also the years when the Government was trying hard to sell to the country the idea of planned development. The Government sought to explain to the MPs—and through

Front page of The Hindu newspaper reporting independent India's first budget.

cept of a fiscal deficit was still about 35 years away—first began to grow. In 1950-51, for instance, John Mathai had actually left a small surplus of a few lakhs. But by 1956-57, when Deshmukh presented his last budget, the deficit had climbed to a dizzying Rs 360 crore, an increase of more than 400 per cent. The reason was forced investment in the First Five-Year Plan. The private sector having failed to mobilise resources, the State was doing the job—largely by borrowing via treasury bills. It was also during this period that a new animal reared its head—the ad hoc treasury bill, an euphemism for printing notes. Slipped in slyly, it would over the years become the most important source of government finance in the 1980s.

BY the end of 1955, it had become clear to Deshmukh, who wasn't a politician and wasn't very good at man management, that he was losing ground in the Cabinet with Jawahar Lal Nehru. The Second Five-Year Plan was just round the corner. The Finance Minister was under pressure from all sides to get on with finding the money to finance it. Sometime in early 1956, Deshmukh decided to go. An opportunity soon presented itself during the reorganisation of states—he took up the cause of Maharashtra against Gujarat and resigned.

With him ended the era of fiscal rectitude, of striving for balanced budgets, of reasonable rates of taxation, of not squeezing the middle class on the grounds of sacrifice for future generations. Brought in as a technocrat, he had to finally give in to the idea of quick growth even if it meant taking India down a path that would lead to several fiscal challenges en route.

It is to that extraordinary story that we now turn, the years of early hope, when nothing seemed impossible, when India's star was on the ascendant. It was to be the great laboratory of economic experiment, the showcase which economists, planners, liberals and well-meaning bureaucrats would hold up with pride to the world.

them to the nation—why planning was necessary and what Five-Year Plans would achieve. But beneath all this there was the constant anxiety: where would the forex come from to finance the plans and would prices remain stable? No clear answers were forthcoming.

It was during those years that the budget deficit—the con-

EXCERPTS FROM THE BUDGET FOR 1948-49

RK SHANMUKHAM CHETTY, FINANCE MINISTER

"When I presented my Interim Budget for Free India's first Parliament a few months back, our nation had been shaken to its very foundations by the great Punjab tragedy...

Our new found freedom, however, weathered the storm, and as the eve of my first annual Budget approached, I could see a silver lining around the cloud. Then, suddenly, like a thunderbolt that rends the sky and spins the globe, calamity struck us once more and orphaned our infant State and enveloped the country with a darkness even more complete. The hand that nailed Jesus to the Cross reached out of the evil recesses of history once again and slew the latest in the line of Prophets. Along with Bernard Shaw one wonders "Must then a Christ Perish in torment in every age to save those that have no Imagination" In Mahatma Gandhi the world has lost an uplifting standard, our nation its Founding Father—and each one of his friend, philosopher and guide. Many ran up to him in times of stress, national or personal, and came back with renewed confidence. Our fledgling freedom felt warm and secure under the protective wing of Gandhiji. The way ill fortune has dogged our heels makes one doubt whether our people had made a tryst with disaster rather than with destiny.

...Western Europe is still in a sad plight... All hope is now centred round the Marshall Plan. But its gestation is unduly delayed, and it has worsened the already strained relations between the Big Three. Over a large part of the world, economic conditions are still worse than in wartime, production has fallen, even below pre-war levels in some cases, and prices have been soaring to new heights. The world food situation is still a cause for serious anxiety...

Independent India's first Minister of Finance RK Shanmukham Chetty

...The food position still continues to cause anxiety and conditions have definitely become worse in large parts of the Madras Presidency following the failure of the monsoon. Steps are being taken to make additional supplies available but the position is bound to be difficult until the new harvest comes on the market....

...In my speech last November I mentioned the rising trend of prices as the most unwholesome feature in our economic situation. This, as I explained then, was the result of a number of factors some of which like the accumulation of surplus purchasing power in the hands of the community, have been in operation for some time while an round fall in production, both industrial and agricultural, was of more recent origin. I stressed then the need for increasing production in every possible way......These difficulties are inherent in the situation but it does not necessarily follow that Government are doing nothing in the matter...

A view that has in recent years become almost unanimous among economists and financiers is that each year a Government's financial policy should be so planned as to rectify the economic maladjustments of the time, and to serve as a compensatory device to offset fluctuations in the private sector of economy... when a depression is on, Government should launch bold schemes of public expenditure and should boldly budget for a deficit if necessary.

...An inflationary pressure resulting from too much money chasing too few goods has been the keynote of our present economy, and there is no indication that a reversal of this trend is in sight. At such a juncture, we should exert every nerve to budget for a surplus, if possible, by increasing revenue and curtailing expenditure....

The methods by which these aims are achieved are important, because as the present phase of inflation is due to an abundance of spending power without the goods to spend on, we must see that a surplus is achieved in such a way as to curtail spending and create suitable incentives for increasing production. In other words, the tax-burdens laid must be met by cutting down expenditure on consumption and not by saying less. Similarly, the borrowing made must be from genuine savings and not from inflated bank credit. The practical application of these principles is indeed difficult, but we must bear them in mind in shaping our financial policy."

The Fiscal Robinhoods

(1957-1969)

The overall objective during this period was clear—raise more money for the Plans.

TT Krishnamachari, Finance
Minister, on his way to the
Parliament House to present the
Budget on March 19, 1957

A S 1956 gave way to 1957, there was a buzz in India. The states had been re-organised, Panchshil and non-alignment had been inaugurated, Nehru was in undisputed command of the country and the Congress held almost a two-thirds majority. The First Plan had been hailed as a great success. The Second was being finalised. The sterling balances were vanishing but only a few officials in the finance and commerce ministries knew it. Foreign donors were queuing up to help India. For them India was the flavour of the decade.

It was in these circumstances and milieu that TT Krishnamachari became the finance minister after Deshmukh's resignation. A successful businessman from the South, TTK was ascerbic, arrogant and often brilliant. More importantly, he enjoyed Nehru's full support. Nehru wanted a huge resource-raising effort for the Second Five-Year Plan from the finance ministry and TTK convinced him that he was the man for the job.

TTK's conduct of the fisc has always been something of a mystery. As a private sector man, moreover one who had run a business well, he knew that Nehru's socialism with the state controls it implied was fraught with the greatest dangers. Yet, it was he who was the author of the Industrial Policy Resolution of 1956 which completely neutered private industry in India by putting it in a straitjacket. But he also started the development financial institutions, IDBI and later, ICICI to help the private sector. As commerce minister, he had been an import hawk. As finance minister, he turned a vociferous import-substitutionist. He believed implicitly in the importance of a sensible interest rate policy and the independence of the RBI. But it was he who intervened in the former and undid the RBI's autonomy.

With such a mercurial man at the helm and that too one who enjoyed the Prime Minister's full support and confidence, it was hardly surprising that the budget for 1957-58 stood everything on its head. In fairness to TTK, though, there was really no other way of financing the Plan or giving effect to the Avadi Congress's directive to capture the commanding heights of the economy. A fiscal revolution was needed and TTK provided it—by raising taxes all round. Most people have subsequently excoriated TTK for not having had the intellectual back-up for adopting the tax policy which he introduced. It was a policy which persisted for nearly 30 years until VP Singh began to dismantle it in 1985.

TTK had an excellent mentor—Lord Nicholas Kaldor. Called in to come up with some bright ideas for financing the plan, Kaldor gave play to his fullest socialist predilections. He was a fiscal Robin Hood, strongly believing in redistribution—and in TTK he found his Friar Tuck. Kaldor proposed that in addition to the income tax, there should be a capital gains tax, a wealth tax, a gift tax and an expenditure tax. This, he said, would close all loopholes—assuming of course that everyone was a hundred per cent honest, there were no delays and that all transactions would be done through the banking system. The officials in the finance ministry were aghast when they heard that TTK was proposing to adopt all these ideas in his Budget. They pointed out to him that even Labour Britain hadn't done, preferring instead to confer a peerage on Kaldor. They lodged a series of strong protests. TTK heard them out, spent a few sleepless nights—and over-ruled them. It was quintessential TTK, the man who thought he knew best.

The immediate consequence of the 1957 Budget which was presented late in May after an interim one in February was a near-total collapse of confidence. The stock market collapsed, the middle class, such as it was in those days took it on the chin and private industry quietly decided that it would stop participating in the national effort. TTK and Nehru had pushed the affluent classes out of the team. Henceforth, it would be the State all the way which would carry the load.

The political mood naturally failed to match the gloom in business and upper middle class society. It was euphoric, believing that the magic key to growth had been found. It seemed right that those who could afford to do so should pay for investment effort. No one, however, asked if too much was not being demanded, both by way of investment and the means to pay for it. The ends justified the means.

But soon after TTK presented his budget, he was assailed by doubts. He went around the major industrial centres reassuring industrialists who told him not without reason, to make available some money to them. TTK listened and ordered the Life Insurance Corporation (LIC), which had by then been nationalised—at his initiative—to buy on a large scale shares in the stock market. The LIC chairman protested but was overruled. One beneficiary of this intervention was businessman Haridas Mundhra who, it turned out later, had sold some dummy shares. This fact came to light. TTK was forced to quit because there was a wholly unwarranted whiff of corruption about him. He was totally honest but so headstrong that he had failed to heed official advice and denied all knowledge of the Mundhra affair. Thus ended—for the time being—a tempestuous debut.

THE 1958-59 budget was presented by Nehru himself who tried to retrieve some of the ground lost in the previous year. But the die had been so firmly cast by TTK that Nehru found himself introducing the gift tax, left out by TTK in the previous year. But Nehru had other things to do and soon handed the finance ministry over to Morarji Desai, who would go on to present the next five budgets, seeing India through the remaining years of the Second Plan which was a great success, the Chinese war which was not, and into the most glorious of all plans, the Third Five-Year Plan.

Morarji, first and foremost, was a politician. In that sense his appointment was a watershed one because until then it

> Morarji Desai introduced a number of new features in the budget. The credit for giving more figures, classifying the budget sensibly, and making it the premier economic document by adopting clear presentational methods goes to him.

had been believed that a finance minister had to be a technocrat or a businessman. All the previous finance ministers had fitted into one or the other of these two categories. As a result, none had had the sort of clout that is required by a finance minister, the sort of clout that comes with an independent political standing. Morarji's greatest asset was his determination and his ability to get his ministerial colleagues to accept his decision which was often a negative one. Ministers would clamour for funds and Morarji would stand firm like a rock. Once his reputation had been established as a no-nonsense man, things became a great deal easier at the finance ministry. His was also the period of consolidation and administrative innovation. He introduced a number of new features in and during the presentation of the budget which have stood the test of time. The credit for giving more figures, classifying the budget more sensibly, and generally making it the premier economic document by adopting clear presentational methods goes to him. Yet, in spite of this his was not a fiscally innovative period. The overall objectives were clear—raise more money for the plans—and the route map had been set out by TTK in 1957. So even though Morarji presented six budgets, and even piloted the new Income Tax Act, he isn't remembered as one of the great finance ministers. His forte was running things sensibly, not changing the system and he did a good job of that. He was an able consolidator, rationaliser and administrator. That is what he set about to do—with outstanding success between 1959 and 1964 when, following the Kamraj Plan which asked all senior Congress ministers to give up office for organisational work, TTK made a comeback.

The results, as we shall see, were once again dramatic.

(Right page) Prime Minister Indira Gandhi lent a patient ear to all the different views on devaluation

THE IDEA OF DEVALUATION

PRIME Minister Indira Gandhi was converted to the idea of a devaluation soon after she assumed office. Yet, anticipating opposition from within her party and the Government in an election year, Indira Gandhi not only chewed patiently on the arguments PC Bhattacharyya and LK Jha gave her in favour of the course, she also invited leading economists to advise her on the implications of the step. In addition, according to the recollections of some officials, she formed a secret committee early in 1966 to examine all options and report about their likely economic consequences...

In March 1966, Indira Gandhi visited the United States. Her visit was preceded by that of a technical mission comprising IG Patel, MR Shroff, and VK Ramaswami which held discussions with the Fund and World Bank...

Discussions of Indian Officials held at the Fund centred largely on the size of a possible rupee devaluation. Some thought had been given to this in India in February, when it was felt that 'an increase of 50 per cent in the rupee value of foreign exchange' was the maximum extent of devaluation necessary...

Some preliminary discussions at the Fund suggested that it would be satisfied with a rate of Rs 6 against the prevailing one of Rs 4.76 for the US dollar...

According to one account whose reliability cannot be verified, Indira Gandhi chose the lower rate (Rs7.50) in the course of a meeting with Schwetizer who reportedly told her that six rupees to the dollar 'would be good. Seven would be better. Seven and a half would be fantastic'.

(Excerpted from History of the Reserve Bank of India, Volume 2, Pp 681-3)

An agreement for the loan of £10 million (Rs 13.33 crore) to the Government of India from British Government was signed in New Delhi on August 26, 1963 by LK Jha, Secretary, Ministry of Finance & Mr R.H. Belsher, Acting British High Commissioner. This constituted a part of the £30 million (Rs 40 crore) loan, offered by Britain as member of Aid India Consortium during 1963-64 to cover their contribution towards the foreign exchange costs of economic development under Third Five-Year Plan.

INTO THE ABYSS

Looking back to that period, it is easy to be full of sombre wisdom. But the fact is that when TTK re-entered the finance ministry late in 1963, India was reeling under a series of hammer blows. The hardest of these was Nehru's ill-health. In October of 1963, he had suffered a stroke and was half incapacitated. The old question—after Nehru, who?—was haunting everyone.

India was also recovering from the disastrous defeat at the hands of the Chinese in October 1962. Its reputation was in tatters, its treasury almost empty and its morale at rock-bottom. Prices were once again starting to rise, forex reserves were dwindling and there was a mood of general dis-satisfaction. The one encouraging feature in this gloomy scenario was the success of the Second Plan and the hopes generated by the Third. It had started off well and, given resources, would end well. All that was needed was money, forex and a bit of luck.

It was in this situation that TTK reclaimed his interrupted reign at the finance ministry. He tried to set the economy on a course which would encourage investment, raise savings, ease the balance of payments problem and, in general restore confidence by reducing the rigours of brutal taxation.

> TTK tried to set the economy on a course which would encourage investment, raise savings, ease the balance of payments problem and, in general restore confidence by reducing the rigours of brutal taxation.

But that was not to be. A few weeks after the budget was presented and before it could be passed, Nehru died on May 27, 1964. The Congress leadership began to conduct an intense succession debate, with the result that much of the fiscal year was a washout. The best that could be hoped for was that there wouldn't be sharp slide into some hidden abyss. The finance ministry itself was being run about as well as it could be under the circumstances but it was a holding operation, with no sense of overall direction and certainly none of the certainties that had abounded a couple of years earlier.

Even so, as India moved into 1965, some of the old optimism started returning. The most important thing was that the system had held itself together after Nehru's death. India had survived as a democracy and would continue to do so. Agricultural output had reached a record of 64 million tonnes. Industrial output was up by 8 per cent. The forex position, though still precarious, was slowly improving. International agencies were bending over backwards to help out, as was the US.

By the time TTK rose to present the budget in February 1965, confidence had been almost fully restored. He even talked of a small surplus on the revenue account. He initiated a voluntary disclosure scheme for black money and set up the machinery that would attack monopolies and concentration of economic power. Reading that speech today, it is hard to tell that just a few weeks earlier the national mood had been so grim and despairing.

But if a week is a long time in politics, a quarter is an eternity in economics. That summer, two things happened which pushed India right off the brink. In June, Pakistan attacked in the Rann of Kutch and was repulsed. Worse still, the monsoon failed. Even before the full enormity of this second disaster had sunk in, Pakistan attacked yet again in September, this time in Kashmir.

The resulting war was a stalemate but the toll it took of public finances sealed the Third Plan's fate. Finally, two and a half months before the fiscal year ended, on January 11, 1966, Prime Minister Lal Bahadur Shastri died of a massive heart attack in Tashkent where he had gone for peace talks with Pakistan.

The fat was now truly in the fire—in a space of 20 months

Prime Minister Lal Bahadur Shastri
with an international delegation

Indo-Pak War (1965): Indian jawans standing guard at the Police Station, Barkee, in the Lahore sector

(Right top) Jammu and Kashmir: Indian security forces fishing out infiltrators

(Right bottom) Pakistani troops in the Rann of Kutch pack their gear and break camp after Cease Fire Agreement in 1965

India had lost two prime ministers, fought two wars which came on top of an earlier one in 1962 and was grappling with a major drought. It was, if you will, a quadruple whammy, ready-made for an economic crisis. And crisis is what India got.

For the next three years, as drought persisted and a balance of payments crisis broke, budgeting would become a joke, planning would be forgotten and politics become a nightmare as the first wave of defection politics hit. Together, all this would ensure that India would, for the remainder of the century, turn into the great lost liberal hope. So overwhelming was the impact of the 1960s disasters that India is yet to recover from it. It was a lost decade not only in terms of lost chances but also in that India lost its mind as well. War, famine, political uncertainty, economic distress, with the cup of misery brimming over, India despairingly turned for succour first to the bureaucracy because it seemed the one national institution that stood between chaos and stability. Then it turned to Indira Gandhi because she promised a new dawn.

Introducng the Final Budget for 1957-58

TT KRISHNAMACHARI, FINANCE MINISTER

INDIRECT TAXATION

"I might begin first with my proposals in the field of indirect taxation. Taking Customs first, it will be appreciated that the scope for raising additional revenues from, them is limited.

Hon'ble Members are aware of the severe restrictions we have imposed on imports in order to curtail our foreign exchange expenditure. Moreover, import duties on most of the so-called luxury articles are already fairly high and the duties on capital goods and industrial raw materials have necessarily to be kept as low as possible. The proposals I have made envisage the raising of the rates of duty by small amounts on about 90 items. I have also taken this opportunity to rationalise the rates in the Customs Tariff which run into several hundred items. There is considerable diversity in these rates which is of no real significance and is in fact administratively cumbrous. I have tried to give the tariff rates a simpler form and in this process the surcharges have been merged into the basic rates. I have also availed myself of this opportunity to convert the rates of duty both in the import and export tariff in terms of decimal coverage. No other change is being made in the export duties. Altogether, my proposals in respect of import duties will yield a revenue of about Rs 6 crore spread over a large number of items, too numerous to mention here.

45. *(Excise Duties)*—I now come to Union Excise Duties. I may say at once that I have fairly substantial proposals under this head, and in doing so, I have in mind the double objective of restraining consumption and of giving a fillip to exports. I propose the following increases:-

(i) *(Motor spirit)*—The existing excise duty which works out at 96 N.P. per Imperial Gallon inclusive of surcharge be raised to 125 N.P. per Imperial Gallon. This will yield an additional revenue of Rs 6.65 crore in a full year.

(ii) *(Refind Diesel Oil)*—The existing duty of 25 N.P. per I.G. be raised to 40 N.P. per I.G. This is estimated to yield Rs 1.90 crore in a full year. (iii) (Diesel oil, not otherwise specified)—The duty be raised from Rs 30 per ton to Rs 40 per ton, the additional yield from which over a year is estimated at Rs 35 lakh.

(iv) *(Kerosene)*—The existing duty of 18.75 N.P. per I.G. be increased fractionally to 20 N.P. per 1.G. This will yield Rs 2 0 lakh in a full year.

(v) *(Cement)*—The existing duty of Rs 5 per ton be raised to Rs 20 per ton, the estimated annual yield being Rs 6.7 crore.

(vi) *(Steel ingots)*—The existing duty of Rs 4 per ton be raised to Rs 40 per ton, yielding on an annual basis Rs 5.7 crore.

(vii) *(Sugar)*—The existing duty of Rs 5.62 per cwt. be raised to Rs 11:25 per cwt. This will yield Rs 18.55 crore in a full year.

(viii) *(Vegetable non-essential oils)*—The duty of Rs 7 0 per ton be raised to Rs 112 per ton. This will mean an increase from about 3 N.P. to 5 N.P. per lb. The estimated yield on this account is Rs 3.15 crore in a year.

(ix) *(Tea)*—The duty be raised as follows:-

    (a) Loose tea-from 6.25 N.P. to 10 N.P. per lb.

    (b) Package tea converted from duty paid loose tea-from 18.7 5 N.P. to 35 N.P. per lb.

    (c) Package tea-from 25 N.P. to 45 N.P. per lb.

    This will yield an additional revenue of Rs 2.45 crore in a year.

(x) *(Coffee)*—The existing duty be raised from 18.75 N.P. per lb. to 35 N.P. per lb., the estimated additional yield being Rs 80 lakh.

(xi) *(Unmanufactured tobacco)*—The duty be raised as under:-

    (a) if other than flue-cured and used for the manufacture of cigarettes or smoking mixtures for pipes and cigarettes-from 56 N.P. per lb. to 75 N.P. per lb.

    (b) if not flue-cured and not actually used for the manufacture of cigarettes or smoking mixtures for pipes and cigarettes and such tobacco cured in whole leaf form and packed or tied in bundles, hanks or bunches or in the form of twists or coils-from 37 N.P. per lb. to 50 N.P. per lb.

    (c) if other than flue-cured and not otherwise specified-from 87 N.P. per lb. to 10 0 N.P. per lb.

The additional yield from these increases aggregates Rs 6.15 crore in a full year.

(xii) *(Matches)*—The existing duties be raised so as to permit of sale of match boxes at 6 N.P. and 4 N.P. per match box of 60's and 40 is respectively. The gain to revenues in full year by these increases is estimated at Rs 6.2 crore.

(xiii) *(Paper)*—My proposals involve an increase in the existing duty on various types of paper the aggregate additional yield being estimated at Rs 2 crore on an annual basis.

46. These proposals in respect of Central Excise Duties are estimated to yield Rs 60.80 crore in a full year. For the remaining part of the current year, their yield is estimated at Rs 53.20 crore, out of which the share of the States will be about Rs 4.2 crore in respect of tobacco and matches.

DIRECT TAXATION

I propose to make certain adjustments in personal income-tax and super-tax rates. ... It is necessary to recognise that the basic rates should apply to the person who earns his income, that is, sweats and toils for it, and that others who derive their income from property and investments, that is, without making any direct effort should be made to pay more by a surcharge...

I propose to impose a higher surcharge on unearned incomes... base. I also propose a revised schedule of these rates and introduce a new scheme of surcharge levy which will mean that the total of the income-tax, super-tax and surcharge for the highest slab will be brought down from the existing level of 91.8 per cent to 84 per cent for unearned and 77 per cent for earned incomes. The surcharge will be 5 per cent on the tax computed at the standard schedule rates for earned incomes up to Rs 1 lakh and 10 per cent on incomes in excess of that sum. For unearned incomes, there will be a uniform surcharge of 20 per cent over the standard schedule rates.

When a person's income is partly earned and partly unearned, the unearned income will be considered to belong to the slab in which the earned income ends and to higher slabs where necessary. The rates for, the lower slabs have been adjusted in keeping with this change in respect of top slabs. To provide relief to the middle classes, I propose that no surcharge on unearned income be levied where the total income does not exceed Rs 7,500. The reduction in the rates of direct taxation will cost the exchequer Rs 71-72 crore. This reduction should, however, be judged in the light of the other changes in direct taxation which I mention later.

52. I propose also to widen the present income-tax base by reducing the taxable minimum from Rs 4,200 to Rs 3,000. The minimum limit had been raised over the past few years mainly for administrative reasons. An income of Rs 4,200, modest though it is in absolute terms, is quite a large multiple of the average level of incomes in the country. It is reasonable to expect that those with an income over Rs 3,000 should also make their contribution, however small, to the public exchequer, and should come within the range of direct taxation...

The wider coverage of income-tax consequent on this set of proposals will bring in about Rs 5 crore this year.

...My next proposal relates to the taxation of Companies. I propose to raise the income-tax payable by Companies from the present level of 4 annas in the rupee to 30 per cent and the

"I propose to impose a higher surcharge on unearned incomes. I also propose a revised schedule of these rates and introduce a new scheme of surcharge... highest slab will be brought down from the existing level of 91.8 per cent to 84 per cent..."

TT Krishnamachari, Finance Minister, Government of India on July 12, 1957.

Corporation Tax from the present level of 2 annas 9 pies in the rupee to 20 per cent. As Hon. Members are aware, shareholders of Companies are entitled to credit of income-tax paid on their behalf by the Company. The net effect of the proposal to increase income-tax on Companies will, therefore, not be very significant. It will to some extent help us to check tax evasion. The need for corporate savings is as great as ever. In view, however, of the increase proposed by me in the rate of Corporation Tax, I propose to reduce the Excess Dividends Tax—to 10 per cent on distribution of dividends between 6 per cent and 10 per cent of the paid-up capital, to 20 per cent on distribu-

tion between 10 per cent and 18 per cent of the paidup capital, and to 30 per cent on the balance.

...My next proposal with regard to Companies relates to the tax on undistributed profits of companies in which the public are not substantially interested. This tax has frequently been the subject matter of considerable argument. The principle on which the tax is based is unexceptionable, namely, that individuals having income in the higher brackets should not be allowed to avoid payment of super-tax by forming close corporations and not distributing their profits in such corporations. However, in the context of our development plans, we have to balance against the need to prevent super-tax avoidance the needs of companies for funds required for expanding industrial activities. I propose to reduce to 45 per cent the minimum percentage of available profits which an industrial company of the above type should distribute in order to avoid the penal consequences of inadequate distribution; for non-industrial companies the percentage will continue to be retained at 60 per cent. For a company which derives profits partly from industrial activities and partly from other activities, the minimum distribution required will be 45 per cent of available industrial profits and 60 per cent of other available profits. Investment companies will be required to distribute 100 per cent as usual. In cases where the accumulated profits and reserves are not less than the paidup capital or the value of the fixed assets, the minimum percentage required to be distributed is at present 100 per cent for all companies. I propose to reduce the percentage to 45 per cent for the industrial companies and 90 per cent for others. With these reductions in the minimum amount required to be distributed, it will be unnecessary to continue the present scheme of adjudication by the Commissioner of Income Tax and the Board of Referees on the business needs of companies seeking total or partial exemption from the operation of the provisions relating to minimum distribution.

The Path to Fiscal Indiscretion

(1970-1979)

This was a period of populism. The price of this was inflations and a balance of payments problem.

The Indian Economic Delegation to America
called on the Prime Minister Indira Gandhi
at Parliament House on April 17, 1969

BAPTISM BY FIRE

After Nehru's death the Congress party's regional bosses installed the diminutive Lal Bahadur Shastri instead as Prime Minister. But in January 1966 he suddenly died and in his place came Indira Gandhi. She was faced with an economic crisis of unprecedented dimensions. Two-thirds of India was hit by drought, which meant that relief works were costing the exchequer dear. Food imports had grown alarmingly which meant that foreign exchange reserves had all but vanished and brutal import controls were in place. The economy had stopped growing for the first time in two decades. Tax receipts were down about 30 per cent of estimates, industrial production was expected to grow by only 6 per cent (but that estimate turned out to be wrong) and exports were growing altogether too slowly for comfort. Prices were rising, the states were being starved of development funds.

Indira Gandhi inherited Sachin Chaudhury as finance minister—TTK having resigned at the end of 1965. Chaudhury made no bones about the economic situation. But the policy response both on the food management side and on the exchange rate side was delayed. Whatever was done came too late in the day to stave off the crisis which, when it broke, took everyone by surprise. 1966 thus drew wearily on, witnessing a politically unpopular devaluation in June, another bad agricultural year with output falling a little, continuing food imports, high inflation of 14 per cent, a bad industrial performance, and the fiscal aftermath of a balance of payments crisis, namely, severe fiscal contraction. The last was hardly surprising considering that the fiscal deficit stood at over 7 per cent of GDP. The inflation and the balance of payments crisis were both a consequence of this.

There are no reliable accounts of the impact of this baptism by fire on Indira Gandhi. But the general consensus is that, along with the finance ministry, she lost faith in both foreign aid and export promotion. Her natural tendency to rely on domestic resources and effort was strongly reinforced by the experience of her first year in office. She was content to leave the running of the economy to civil servants while she busied herself with the party, the forthcoming general election and foreign policy.

The bureaucratic response was to batten down hatches and get into a siege mentality. This engendered further controls and limitations on freedoms of action which, when external new shocks came, made it difficult for the economy to adjust quickly enough on its own, without further interventions by the government. India turned into a virtual autarky. But even after conceding that the civil servants only made the best of a terrible situation in the absence of a clear political direction, the question needs to be asked if, given the short duration of the crisis and its origin in an external shock (drought), the fiscal reaction that followed was not excessive. There have been many subsequent studies which suggest precisely this. They point out that the sharp cutbacks in public investment that followed the crisis of 1965-67 only succeeded in making India more vulnerable and prone to the series of shocks that followed in the 1970s.

THE PARADIGM SHIFTS

Morarji Desai, who became finance minister in 1967 was a fiscal conservative of the old school who believed in balanced budgets. India had just been through a deeply wounding crisis, he said, which meant that this wasn't the time for experimentation and adventurism. Controls, he said, were not desirable but would have to be tightened lest things went wrong again. High taxes acted as disincentives but, equally, there was a pressing need to meet the needs of effective governance. So he raised the overall levels of taxation, especially of the direct sort. Imports are ordinarily a sign of a booming economy but not just now, he said, further tightening import controls. Exports should increase, he repeated, even as

(Top) Morarji Desai, who became Finance Minister in 1967, with an international delegation. (from bottom right)) Jaiprakash Narayan who mounted a strong opposition to Indira Gandhi; C Subramaniam who was Finance Minister during the heydays of Emergency; YB Chawan who presented a mini budget in 1974

he built in a bias in policy against them via export duties. By any token, the three budgets between 1967 and 1969 were extraordinary examples of saying one thing and doing the opposite. Bearing the stamp of a conservative bureaucracy and an old-fashioned finance minister, they achieved nothing of significance. Many would argue that they well and truly laid the foundations of the licence-quota-permit-control raj that was to shackle the economy in the coming two decades.

Soon after presenting the budget for 1969, Morarji Desai resigned over the issue of "social" control of banks (14 of which were later nationalised in July). Within a few months, the political crisis which had been brewing for about a year, finally broke on the Congress party. In July that year, the party split into two factions, one led by Indira Gandhi as the young turk and the other by the Old Gang, now portrayed as a bunch of politicians who stood between prosperity and the masses. Just how determined she was to win the political battle was brought home to the nation when she rose to present the budget for 1970-71 on February 28, 1970.

For the first time since independence, the budget became an instrument of politics. Until that last day of February in 1970, the budget had been a tool devoted to, and designed for, the economy alone. The idea that it could be used to project the Congress party as a saviour of the poor never crossed anyone's mind. Politics did intervene from time to time but only tangentially. Nehru had been too honest a politician to allow the budget to be used for party political purposes. It was, he made it clear, to be used for gaining purely economic objectives.

So when taxes were raised, the Government didn't go to town saying it was in order to redistribute wealth or to at-

> The budget became an instrument of politics. Until then it was a tool devoted to, and designed for, the economy alone. The idea that it could be used to project the Congress party as a saviour of the poor never crossed anyone's mind.

tack poverty "directly", whatever that meant. It simply said that higher taxes were necessary to pay for such and such investments in plant and machinery or for meeting such and such contingent liability. Aware of the implications of introducing issues relating to the redistribution of wealth into the budget, until 1970, governments consciously avoided linking distributional issues to the budget. It was, until Indira Gandhi changed it, simply a document of housekeeping with a few remarks about the state of house thrown in. Indira Gandhi's defenders say that it was all right for Nehru to walk the straight and narrow path as the Congress never faced any sort of challenge until 1967. But once the challenge arose—both within and outside the party—it became impossible to avoid using whatever weapons were at hand. After all, she only changed the emphasis and pattern of expenditure from industrial investment to rural areas via the poverty alleviation programmes. This had the merit of bringing the poverty question bang into the centre of the policy debate.

THE ERA OF POPULISM

From 1970 to 1974, the economy turned sharply left. Indira Gandhi set the tone. Listen to her words, as she presented her first—and only—budget in 1970:

"The provision of adequate employment opportunities is not just a welfare measure. It is a necessary part of the strategy of development in a poor country which can ill-afford to keep any resources unutilised or under-utilised. Greater attention to dry farming areas is not merely to avoid inequalities in the rural areas. It is also an essential part of any programme to achieve

Mr Robert S McNamara, the President of the World Bank in conversation with IG Patel, Economic Secretary, Ministry of Finance in New Delhi, Januray 24, 1972

sustained increases in agricultural production. Encouragement to small enterprises and to new entrepreneurs is vital to build up managerial and entrepreneurial talent which is all too scarce today. Without some restraint on urban land values and individual ownership of urban property, we cannot adequately develop housing and other amenities required to wrest the maximum benefits from the vast productive investments already made in our over-crowded towns and cities. The weakest sections of the society are also the greatest source of potential strength. We cannot provide for all the urgent needs of society with our limited resources. But a balance has to be struck between outlays which may be immediately productive and those which are essential to create and sustain a social and political framework which is conducive to growth in the long run.

"I would like to say that in presenting my first Budget to this Honourable House, I have become acutely aware of the challenges as well as the constraints of the contemporary epoch of development of our national economy. I (have) endeavoured to set out the broad framework within which this Budget is cast. That framework, I believe, is consistent with the politi-cal, economic and social realities of our country. Convinced as I am of its essential soundness, there is no alternative but to tread a difficult but determined course. If the opportunities for growth which are so much in evidence are to be seized fully, no effort must be spared for raising resources for the purpose. To flinch from this effort at this stage would be to impose even heavier burdens in the years to come. If we allow the present momentum of growth to wane for the sake of some purely temporary advantage, we will deny ourselves the cumulative benefits of a higher rate of growth for all time to come. If the requirements of growth are urgent, so is the need for some selective measures of social welfare. The fiscal system has also to serve the ends of greater equality of incomes, consumption and wealth, irrespective of any immediate need for resources. At the same time, the needs of those sectors of the economy which require private initiative and investment must also be kept in mind in the interest of growth of the economy as a whole. I can only hope that the proposals I have just presented steer clear of the opposite dangers of venturing too little or attempting too much."

Thus began a process of competitive populism. But in 1970, for a country looking for a fresh whiff of leadership, new ideas and desperate for reassurance that someone was at last in charge, these ideas came as a clarion call comparable only to the "tryst with destiny" speech of Nehru 23 years earlier.

The full force of the Government's new determination to launch a "direct attack on poverty" became evident when income taxes were raised to extraordinarily high levels—the marginal rate went up to 97 per cent and along with the incidence of wealth tax, over a 100 per cent. Indirect taxes were also hiked, especially on things which the government regarded as being luxuries or inessential. Outlays for rural development were increased sharply. Exchange control was tightened, as was industrial licensing.

EMPLOYMENT schemes were inaugurated with much fanfare. The newly nationalised banks were asked to go rural, regardless of profitability. Small scale industry received its share of the largesse as well. It was a complete reversal of the fiscal conservatism of the previous quarter of a century. And as such, it was only a matter of time before a crisis hit. The ingredients were there. All that was needed was a shock to the system. And it came soon enough. In 1972, the monsoon failed and in October 1973 Iran quadrupled oil prices.

The fiscal crisis of 1973-74 acted as a dampener on the re-distributive zeal of the Government. Fiscal adventurism was quickly given up and tried and tested methods of restoring order were brought into full play. Inflation was the chief political enemy—as befits a poor country with low per capita incomes. It was tamed by inducing savage cuts in aggregate demand. The counter-productive taxation regime was reversed and the marginal tax rate was brought down to a "mere" 77

> The fiscal crisis of 1973-74 acted as a dampener on the re-distributive zeal of the government. Fiscal adventurism was quickly given up and tried and tested methods of restoring order were brought into full play

per cent. A couple of years later, under the influence of Sanjay Gandhi, it would be further lowered to 66 per cent, where it stayed for 15 years.

Halfway through 1974, it had become clear that Mrs Gandhi had learnt her economic lessons, namely, that the price of excessive populism was inflation and, with bad luck, even a balance of payments problem. In July 1974, YB Chavan presented a mini-budget aimed at eliminating inflation and its main focus was a deep cutting of expenditure, both by direct and indirect means. But the Opposition had seen the possibilities and it would reach dizzying heights of populism when it came to power in 1977.

However, that was still about five years away. Between 1975 and 1979 when Prime Minister Charan Singh presented his disastrous budget fiscal conservatism was the rule. In spite of the momentous political developments which overtook the country—the imposition of Emergency by Indira Gandhi in June 1975, the mass arrests of Opposition politicians, the suspension of habeas corpus, the mass sterilisations, censorship, the amendments to the Constitution—the budgets of those years reveal nothing except caution and good housekeeping.

When one reads nothing but the budget speech of C Subramaniam, finance minister in 1976 when the Emergency was at its height, there is no clue of the police state which had been inaugurated. Even the Janata Party's first budget presented in May 1977 after Indira Gandhi as well as her Congress were defeated in the general election of March, contained no real hint of what had happened in the previous 20 months.

The finance minister was HM Patel, an old ICS Mandarin and the prime minister was Morarji Desai. Both were steeped in old values and ensured, not only that the budget would not become a political tool, but also that it would not be allowed to depart from traditional formats, precepts and practice. Left to themselves, the two would have also ensured lower levels of deficit financing by decontrol and better pricing policies for the public sector. But because it was coalition, cobbled together in haste to defeat Indira Gandhi, the government had a fair share of socialists. They had tasted fiscal blood and would not allow decontrol and sensible price policies.

The result, until 1979, was a continuation of the old policies of fiscal conservatism coupled with arbitrary taxation designed only to raise revenues without much concern for a coherent economic strategy behind them. The finance ministry simply did whatever it wanted. There was never any question of consultation or thinking out a broad strategy of growth. That part was left to the Planning Commission.

Needless to say, the budget deficit rose sharply in these years. So strong was the commitment to planned development and so strong was the suspicion of markets, that even a non-Congress government was unable to shed the old ways. It simply carried on as before, pausing only to raise plan outlays as though this was the way its performance would be judged.

BY serendipity foreign exchange reserves rose during this period in spite of the policy of slow import liberalisation. Mainly, it was the inward remittances from workers in the Gulf that contributed. But exports also grew. On the whole, however, such economic strategy as there was, was made by the Planning Commission which, as in the old days, simply informed the finance ministry that it needed so much and would the Ministry please raise the required amount.

Given that resources were being allocated not by the market but by civil servants, politicians and economists—in that

> Between 1975 and 1979 when Prime Minister Charan Singh presented his disastrous budget fiscal conservatism was the rule. The budgets of those years reveal nothing except caution and good housekeeping .

order—this was perhaps inevitable. As John Mathai had foreseen in 1950—he had preferred to resign as finance minister—there simply wasn't all that much for the finance ministry to do except raise revenues. The spending decisions were taken elsewhere in the ministries which had now proliferated.

So, in a sense, the process which Indira Gandhi had begun at the very start of the decade in 1970, was brought to its culmination in its last year, 1979. The Janata government, after an excellent spell, was in its death throes because of in-fighting led by its own Deputy Prime Minister, Chaudhary Charan Singh who had become Finance Minister. He had before him the example set by Indira Gandhi and decided to use it for his own political benefit.

Ignoring Morarji's advice, in February 1979 he came up with a budget that had a simple message: "I am a farmer, so the budget will tilt towards farmers by soaking the rich and the middle classes". Subsidies to farmers doubled and were financed by significantly higher taxation. But not all of the new largesse could be paid for by new taxes. So, for the first time, a deficit of over Rs 1,000 crore—Rs 1,365 crore—was left uncovered, to be financed by the printing of notes via the issue of ad hoc treasury bills. By the end of the fiscal year, it ballooned to Rs 2,700 crore. It was a trend which would be reversed only briefly during the 1980s. For much of that decade, India would inflate its way to growth—with wholly predictable consequences at the end of the decade. But the political target had been set. India had to break out of the 3.5 per cent Hindu rate of growth syndrome that had persisted for three decades.

By the end of 1979, thanks to high oil prices and inflation, all the good work of the previous five years was undone. India was in crisis once again.

A Reason to Rejoice: a
bumper crop thanks to the
Green Revolution

Introducing the Final Budget for 1970-71

INDIRA GANDHI, PRIME MINISTER and MINISTER OF FINANCE

DIRECT TAXATION

22. The marginal rates of income taxation will be increased progressively on all personal incomes above Rs 40,000 per year. With the addition of the surcharge at 10 per cent, the maximum rate of 93.5 per cent will now be reached in the slab over Rs 2 lakh as against 82.5 per cent, in the slab over Rs 2.21 lakh at present.

23. Simultaneously, the existing rates of ordinary wealth tax are being, enhanced. At present, these rates vary from 0.5 per cent to 3 per cent. They will now vary from 1 per cent at the lowest slab to 5 per cent at the highest slab. For the individual, who derives his entire income from wealth, the combined effect of income and wealth taxation, as now proposed, will impose an effective ceiling on income after tax, when such income reaches approximately Rs 25,000 per annum. On the other hand, there will be an inbuilt incentive in favour of earned incomes. When income is wholly earned, for example, there will be no absolute ceiling, as the highest marginal tax of 93.5 per cent will leave some room for increase in income after tax at all levels.

24. Honourable Members are aware that we are at present examining practical means of imposing a ceiling on urban property. While the legal and other aspects of the matter are being examined, it is proposed to increase the additional wealth tax on urban lands and buildings, so that the objective of a ceiling on urban property is achieved, at least in part, within the framework of the powers already available to the Centre. At present, the additional wealth tax on urban lands and buildings is leviable, in the case of individuals and Hindu undivided families, on the value of lands and buildings situated in cities and towns with a population exceeding one lakh and with an initial exemption ranging from Rs 4 to Rs 7 lakh in different categories of cities.

The tax is leviable on the balance at rates ranging from 1 per cent to 4 per cent. The maximum rate is reached when the value of urban lands and buildings exceeds Rs 19 to Rs 22 lakh. It is now proposed to levy a tax of 5 per cent on the value of urban lands and buildings in excess of Rs 5 lakh and at the rate of 7 per cent on the value in excess of Rs 10 lakh. No distinction will be made in regard to the exemption on the basis of the population of the area, in which the properties are situated. The definition of an urban area is also being enlarged to include areas within the limits of any municipality or other similar authority having a population of 10, 000 or more, with powers to cover by notification areas up to 8 kilometres outside such limits.

Business premises will continue to be excluded from the proposed levy as at present.

However, guest houses maintained by those liable to pay this tax will not be reckoned as business premises. Provisions are also being made to prevent avoidance of the tax by transfer, from individual or joint Hindu family ownership, to ownership by partnership firms, associations of persons and closely-held companies. Another measure which is intended to serve a similar purpose, provides for the taxation of capital gains arising from the sale or transfer of agricultural land situated within urban areas.

55. Sir, before I conclude, I should like to say that in presenting my first Budget to this Honourable House, I have become acutely aware of the challenges as well as the constraints of the contemporary-epoch of development of our national economy. At the very beginning of my speech, I endeavoured to set out the broad framework within which this Budget is cast. That framework, I believe, is consistent with the political, economic and social realities of our country. Convinced as I am of its essential soundness, there is no alternative but to tread a difficult but determined course. If the opportunities for growth which are so much in evidence are to be seized fully, no effort must be spared in raising resources for the purpose. To flinch from this effort at this stage would be to impose even heavier burdens in the years to come. If we allow the present momentum of growth to wane for the sake of some purely temporary advantage, we will deny ourselves the cumulative benefits of a higher rate of growth for all time to come. If the requirements of growth are urgent, so is the need for some selective measures of social welfare. The fiscal system has also to serve the ends of greater equality of incomes, consumption and wealth, irrespective of any immediate need for resources. At the same time, the needs of these sectors of our economy which require private initiative and investment must also be kept in mind in the interest of the growth of the economy as a whole. I can only hope that the proposals I have just presented steer clear of the opposite dangers of venturing too little or attempting too much.

Hundreds of rickshaw pullers representing Janta Auto Rickshaw Sangh and Delhi Cycle Rickshaw Chalak Union were among those who called on the Prime Minister, Indira Gandhi, at her house in New Delhi on July 22, 1969 to congratulate her on the nationalisation of 14 major banks

In Search of Growth

(1980-1990)

The Government decided to pursue growth through heavy deficit financing without paying too much attention to structural reform which would have, to some extent, negated the effects of the higher deficits

MISSED OPPORTUNITIES

In January 1980, Indira Gandhi was back as Prime Minister once again. She chose as her finance minister R Venkataraman, a former labour leader from Tamil Nadu who had some previous experience at the state level of the finance department. He, too, by nature was a conservative and given to fiscal caution.

The times could not have been worse. Inflation was running at 22 per cent. Forex reserves, thanks to the second oil crisis of 1979-80, had all but vanished. There was an unprecedented drought in the country—no famine though, a fact which went unnoticed then. The Sixth Five-Year Plan had to be finalised and resources had to be found for it.

There was no room for manoeuvre so there was no major change in the economic paradigm that had been designed by Indira Gandhi in 1970. If anything, within the limited means available, it sharpened that paradigm's contours, inasmuch as an increasing proportion of investment continued to be poured into the so-called social schemes which had no commercial or economic significance.

So except for undoing the damage done by Charan Singh as far as income tax rates were concerned—he had raised it to the equivalent of a maximum of 72 per cent—the Budget for 1980-81 was essentially a fire-fighting one, designed to contain the budget deficit and the deficit on the current account. The latter had gone from 0.3 per cent of GDP in 1979-80, to 3 per cent in 1980-81. The revised estimates for 1979-80 had shown that the budget deficit had come to an unprecedented Rs 2,700 crore, double of what was estimated a year earlier. This was thanks mainly to the relief works occasioned by the drought and poor tax collections occasioned by the collapse of governance in the middle half of fiscal 1979.

But any expectations that the fiscal contraction of 1980-81 would resolve the twin-crisis of high inflation and a high current account deficit were short-lived. By October 1981 there was only one way out left: a loan from the IMF from its Extended Financing Facility (the non-conditionality credit lines had already been tapped) in order to insulate the Sixth Plan's investments from debilitating shortages of foreign exchange.

This was arranged for in November of 1981 and, helped by a good monsoon and sensible monetary policies, the crisis was a thing of the past by the beginning of the next financial year. Inflation was down to the high single digits, the IMF loan had given some breathing space for imports, exports were starting to pick up, oil prices had stabilised and, more importantly, in order to protect its external economic flanks, India had turned to the USSR for succour. It was time to get on with the tasks of triggering growth and making Indian industry competitive.

It was also the ideal time to globalise. The rest of the world was also coming out of the recession of 1979-82 and helped by Ronald Reagan's huge budget deficits, US imports, were beginning to burgeon. The European market was expanding and Japan was growing as rapidly as ever. With India's large industrial base, its political stability, its record of fiscal prudence and good governance, it was ideally placed.

Instead, it missed the chance altogether. Indeed, it didn't even try. So rigid had become the old mindset, so firm were the convictions about export pessimism and so strong was the grip of the bureaucracy and the other vested interests that, far from taking advantage, India actually retreated behind the shadows. The familiar was more comfortable, the known devil preferable. Excessive caution—dubbed as abundant prudence in the wake of the Latin American debt crisis—ruled the day. While everyone else forged ahead, India remained content in its old certainties.

The Government tried to stimulate growth by priming the pump but even this was not properly done. What India got, instead, was a severe worsening of public finances without the reward of structural reform which could have acted as the platform for the huge fiscally expansionary policies that were to follow.

Madhu Dandavate, the Finance Minister, addressing the Chief
Executives of All India Financial Institutions in New Delhi on
January 21, 1990. The then Finance Secretary Bimal Jalan (on his
right) and RN Malhotra the then RBI Governor.

Prime Minister Rajiv Gandhi giving
the final touches to the 1987-88
budget in New Delhi. Standing
on his side is the then Finance
Secretary S Venkitaramanan

Rajiv Gandhi arriving in Parliament on February 28, 1987 to present the Budget

All that the ministries had to do was to come up with schemes that would pay electoral dividends.

There were exceptions, of course, such as the railways and the energy industry. It had become evident that, thanks to the slower pace of investment in the vital infrastructure industries during the years 1966-75, a huge gap had grown between demand and supply. The permissive political climate had affected productivity and efficiency also. So by the end of the 1970s, not only had a yawning demand-supply gap emerged in these industries but their productivity had also fallen precipitously. These industries were given generous dollops of funds but the all-important need for structural reform—which the IMF loan had made possible—was not addressed. Instead, the approach was the old one—of equating good economic performance with higher plan allocations.

IN the late seventies and early eighties, India's balance of payments situation was a matter of concern. In the budget of 1982-83 presented by the Finance Minister, Pranab Mukherjee, which was the first budget presented by him, the Government's strategy for restoring the viability in our balance of payments was indicated. The main elements of the strategy were to accelerate the pace of import substitution in critical sectors such as oil and fertilisers, to increase exports, and to improve the facilities available for remittances and investments by non-residents of Indian origin. The Government achieved considerable success in implementing this strategy.

There were substantial increases in domestic production of petroleum and fertilisers which enabled India to reduce its dependence on imports of these items. Imports of steel, non-ferrous metals, and several other items

Domestic production of petroleum and fertilisers increased substantially which enabled India to reduce its dependence on imports of these items. Imports of steel, non-ferrous metals, and several other items were also lower.

were also lower. The import policy adopted sought to combine the objective of reducing the growth of imports with the need to continue the liberal access to raw materials and capital goods for priority sectors. Tariff policies were effectively used to provide further protection to indigenous industries. Exports, which increased at the rate of 16 per cent in 1981-82, showed a further growth of 18 per cent in the first seven months of 1982-83. This was a good performance considering the uncongenial external environment marked by rising protectionism, demand recession and near stagnation in world trade.

FISCAL PROFLIGACY

The forward-looking Rajiv Gandhi who succeeded Indira Gandhi was aware that India was getting left behind. He was acutely aware of how far the others had gone and how quickly even East Asian countries were growing. He gave a clear political direction: get on with growth and try and do it with supply-side policies. Taxes were cut steeply, imports were liberalised, the rigours of industrial licensing were eased and, up to a point, the job of resource allocation was entrusted to the markets. The markets responded well and a primary issue boom started which, with a few interruptions, would continue unabated for almost the next decade. A new era had at last arrived—or so it seemed. Encouraged by the higher GDP growth rates achieved during 1983 and 1984, the Government decided to pursue growth through heavy deficit financing without paying too much attention to structural reform which would have, to some extent, negated the effects of the higher deficits. In any case, the advice being tendered, to the political

BUDGET FOR 1984-85

PRANAB MUKHERJEE, FINANCE MINISTER

...Let me now turn to the external payments situation facing the economy. In my budget speech last year, I had informed the House of the improvement that had taken place in our balance of payments in 1982-83. I am happy to say that this improvement has gained strength in 1983-84.

The trade gap, which declined from Rs 5800 crore in 1981-82 to about Rs 5500 crore in 982-83, is expected to decline further in the current year. Receipts on invisibles account have remained buoyant and the incentives for non-resident deposits have been highly successful. Our foreign exchange reserves, Inclusive of IMF drawings, have increased by Rs 662 crore in the current financial year upto 10th February...

Our strategy for bringing the balance of payments under control, after the sharp deterioration that occurred in 1979-80, has paid rich dividends. In view of the improvement in our payments position, the Government has voluntarily decided not to avail of the balance of 1.1 billion SDR under the Extended Fund Facility of the IMF.

While intervening in the debate on the IMF loan in this House in December, 1981, the Prime Minister had this to say, and I quote:

"It does not force us to borrow, nor shall we borrow unless it is in the national interest. There is absolutely no question of our accepting any programme which is incompatible with our policy, declared and accepted by Parliament. It is inconceivable that anybody should think that we would accept assistance from any external agency which dictates terms which are not in consonance with such policies. This was true then, and it is true now."

Belying the prophecies of doom by many a self-styled Cassandra, the economy has emerged stronger as a result of the adjustment effort mounted by us.

None of the dire consequences that we were being warned about has occurred. We have not cut subsidies. We have not cut wages. We have not compromised on planning.

We have not been trapped in a debt crisis. We have not faltered in our commitment to anti-poverty programmes or the welfare of our people. We entered into this loan arrangement with our eyes open. We have come out of it with our heads high.

We hope that our decision to forgo the balance of the amount available to us under the IMF loan would, in a small way, help the IMF to provide greater assistance to other developing countries. I must also take this opportunity to express our appreciation for the goodwill and mutual-understanding that has marked our relationship with the IMF during the entire period of the EFF arrangement....

Four years ago, my distinguished predecessor, while presenting the first Budget of the present Government, had expressed our firm resolve to repair the damage and restore the country's economy to the path of stability, growth and social justice.

Mr Speaker, we have kept that promise.

leadership was such that at least, there seemed no special reason to combine structural reform with fiscal expansion. It wasn't even willing to acknowledge that an opportunity was being missed.

The Government granaries were full, so food imports were not envisaged. Inflation had stabilised at around 7 per cent. The current account deficit was under control and forex reserves were adequate to finance all but the worst of external shocks. A new team was in place and there was euphoria in the air. 1986 removed all doubts as to the strategy that the government was going to follow. The budget carried forward the process begun in 1985 by cutting taxes further, liberalizing imports, reducing tariffs (albeit marginally by current standards) and pumping in more money into the system. Better tax compliance and stiff tax administration, it was argued, would solve minor hiccups along the way.

IN January 1987, Rajiv Gandhi took over the finance ministry himself and Feburary reduced a lot of excise duties and customs and left an uncovered deficit of nearly Rs 6,000 crore which came on top of the nearly Rs 6,000 crore of deficits of the previous two years. In other words, in three years, that is, at the end of fiscal 1987 (which was March 31, 1988) the Government—if it was lucky—would have run up a budget deficit of Rs 12,000 crore. This was more than the combined deficit of years 1970-84.

Could such high deficits be sustained? The Government certainly seemed to think so. It did nothing whatsoever to pay attention to the warnings that were being sounded, especially on the current account deficit. This was gradually widening and, had the exchange rate been adjusted fast enough,

> **Granaries were full, so food imports were not envisaged. Inflation had stabilised at around 7 per cent. The current account deficit was under control and forex reserves were adequate to finance all but the worst of external shocks.**

could have been brought under control through even higher exports (which had been growing pretty satisfactorily at about 12 per cent in dollar terms during the previous three years). But luck, soon ran out. There was a huge drought.

So severe was it that by the end of September 1987 it had become clear that India would have to go in for large scale maintenance imports (of items like edible oils, sugar etc). But the foreign exchange position was none-too-good. But given the situation, the ministry was compelled to go for as much short term debt as was necessary to finance imports. This started India off down the road which would leave it to face a balance of payment crisis in the summer of 1991.

In 1988, Rajiv Gandhi, under political pressure, decided that the biggest dividends were to be had from large government handouts to all potential vote banks. The budget deficit for 1988-89 rose to Rs 8853 crore. 1989 was an election year and and the budget deficit soared to Rs 12149 crore. Over the decade, the wheel had once again come round full circle. Strong action was needed but not taken. Government expenditure kept running away. By 1991, the government was headed into an internal debt trap as its interest payments on ever-increasing borrowings ballooned. In 1992, these payments accounted for a quarter of all government revenues and the proportion was rising.

Externally, the short-term creditors were getting restive and beginning to take their money out. Inflation, at around 15 per cent was once again out of control. By early 1991 forex reserves had come down to just $1.1 billion, enough to cover, with every sort of import restriction, a mere five weeks of imports. India was obliged to mortgage its gold to the Bank of England and impose savage import restrictions.

Introducng the Budget for 1985-86

VISHWANATH PRATAP SINGH, FINANCE MINISTER

Sir,

I deem it a great privilege to present the first Budget of the new Government. I am reminded of the words of our beloved departed leader, the late Prime Minister Smt. Indira Gandhi:

"No section of our vast and diverse population should feel forgotten. Their neglect is our collective loss." We can no longer hear her voice, but her words will live with us. In the task of nation-building, she spared herself no pain—not even the pain of death. She has left us a legacy signed in her own blood; a legacy to preserve this country and keep it moving ahead. To this cause of hers we rededicate ourselves.

The formulation of the Budget is an annual exercise but, to be meaningful, it has to be set in a longer time frame... over the years, objective conditions have changed calling for new responses... we have to initiate a process of reform which can be completed in a phased manner in a time bound frame... In the area of direct taxes, an important priority is to create an environment for growth, productivity and savings. The system of direct taxation which can help in achieving these objectives will also secure better tax compliance, and will be more equitable.

My proposals for the current year in the area of corporate taxation are designed to introduce a directional change by discontinuing certain exemptions and rationalising the rates. For the present, I am not going all the way partly be-

VP Singh addressing a rally

cause of revenue considerations and partly because I would like to watch the response to the changes being proposed now.

In respect of indirect taxes, my immediate task is to bring about changes which would help in reducing costs of investment in priority sectors, encourage the growth of the small-scale sector and remove certain other distortions. During the course of the year, I shall be giving consideration to other changes that might be required for the indirect tax system to make its full contribution to the further development of our economy.

I propose to raise the exemption limit for personal income taxation from Rs 15,000 to Rs

18,000. As a result, out of about 40 lakh assessees, around 10 lakh will not have to pay any income-tax...After the nil rate slab of Rs 18,000, the rate of income-tax on the slab of Rs 18,001 to Rs 25,000 will be 25 per cent; on the slab of Rs 25,001 to Rs 50,000, the rate will be 30 per cent; on the slab of Rs 50,001 to Rs 1 lakh, the rate will be 40 per cent; and on the income in excess of Rs 1 lakh, the rate will be 50 per cent. The new rate schedule will result in a reduction in tax at all levels of income...the maximum marginal rate of income tax on personal incomes will stand reduced from 61.875 per cent to 50 per cent in fact, the average rate of tax would be even lower.

...I am of the view that estate duty has not achieved the twin objectives with which it was introduced, namely, to reduce unequal distribution of wealth and assist the States in financing their development schemes. While the yield from estate duty is only about Rs 20 crore, its cost of administration is relatively high. I, therefore, propose to abolish the levy of estate duty in respect of estates passing on deaths occurring on or after 16th March, 1985. I will come forward in due course with suitable legislation for this purpose.

Let me end, Mr Speaker, as I began, with the words of the late Prime Minister, Smt. Indira Gandhi: "We all have faith in new India. Let us put our shoulder to the wheel".

[16th March, 1985]

India Rising but Slowly

(1991 onwards)

The gradualist pace of reforms meant that it took time to have effect. Yet, the fruits of this effort have been amply evident in the past several years. The average growth rate of the economy was around 4 per cent per year before the 1980s. It increased to an average of about 8 per cent since 2004

SINGH'S DEVALUATION MANTRA

In 1991, India ran headlong into its worst fiscal and balance of payments crisis to date. As though the economic fundamentals were not enough to contribute to the crisis, Rajiv Gandhi was brutally assassinated in May. The resulting political uncertainty contributed to hasten the crash and, by June 1991, India was well and truly bankrupt. The fiscal deficit had ballooned to nearly 9 per cent of GDP; the current account deficit had gone to almost 3 per cent of it; there was a flight of capital from India; and confidence plummeted to depths hitherto unimagined.

Dr Manmohan Singh, the new Finance Minister, had spent a decade in government before moving to the RBI as Governor and then to the Planning Commission as its Deputy Chairman. He thus understood how the government functioned. He also had an understanding of how the global economy had changed and how far India had been left behind.

Dr Singh devalued the rupee in two steps of 16 and 6 per cent, slashed export subsides and mostly abolished industrial licensing. And all this was done even before the budget had been presented in July. The need of the hour was clear: cut the fiscal deficit cut the current account deficit from 2.8 per cent to about one per cent. This meant cutting both imports and government expenditure.

The axe fell, as it always does, on investment expenditure and expenditure on the social sectors like health, education, defence and subsidies. But because of strong resistance within the Congress party, subsidies were soon restored. He was bitterly criticised in Cabinet for his fertiliser subsidy policy and thereafter much to his disappointment it was decided to restore it. Recently he had disclosed that he had resigned over the issue but his resignation was not accepted and he was persuaded to stay.

Dr Singh also had to send out a clear message that India was both reforming and liberalising. So customs duties and excise duties both were cut, direct taxes rationalised and foreign investment given an unmistakable invitation. The general tenor and approach was thus remarkably similar to independent India's first budget of November 1947.

Dr Singh's tenure partially achieved what he had been brought in to do, namely, restore fiscal order. In 1991, Singh had set himself a mental target of taking the fiscal deficit back to the level of the 1970s, around four per cent of GDP. But when he left office, it was still running at over 5.5 per cent of GDP. His other achievements—of liberalisation of trade and investment, of financial sector reform, privatisation, of agreeing not to monetise deficits etc—were politically costless.

PALANI'S PRIDE

The man who took over from Manmohan Singh after the Congress party was defeated was Palaniappan Chidambaram. A committed reformer, he had to work with 12 other parties, including the Communists. As such, he had even less elbow room than did his predecessor. He brought down the maximum rate of income tax to 30 per cent, cut the corporation tax to 40 per cent and reduced the average level of tariffs to just a shade over 25 per cent. As supply-side stimuli go, no one could have asked for more. But the fiscal deficit remained stubbornly high at nearly 8 per cent.

> Manmohan Singh devalued the rupee in two steps of 16 and 6 per cent, slashed export subsides and mostly abolished industrial licensing. And all this was done even before the budget had been presented in July.

Union Finance Minister Manmohan Singh giving final touches to the 1993-94 Budget

DOLDRUMS TO HIGH WINDS

And it would remain so for sometime. But the deficit, although problematic, was not the most pressing problem. The industrial growth rate, which had touched dizzying heights a few years before, had collpased and had to be revived. The tax cuts worked for a while but soon ran out of steam. Overall growth remained sluggish, thanks to the slowdown in industry.

Then in 1997 two other blows came, seemingly out of nowhere. One was domestic, when the National Front government collpased; the other was external, when the Asian economies collapsed. Together, these two unconnected events ensured that the economy would remain stuck in the low growth groove for the next five years. The Government, by now being run a new coalition, the National Democratic Alliance (NDA) did its best but nothing helped. The RBI under Bimal Jalan had turned extra-cautious, so not only was foreign exchange hard to come by, interest rates remained high. It was only after the Asian crisis had definitively by-passed India and George Bush was elected President of the US in 2000, that the RBI began to loosen up.

By 2003, the effects of a tight fiscal policy and gradually loosening monetary policy were beginning to have their effect. Growth returned after almost a decade. India started to become like a debutante at the global ball which was just starting under the amazingly loose fiscal and monetary policies of the US. Purchasing power was flooding the world and this time, unlike in the 1980s, India was there to cash in. For the next five years, dollars poured in, the savings rate shot up and India would grow and grow and grow. It was a heady feeling, to be competing with China's double digit

> All good things must come to an end. In 2008, the global financial crisis struck. The Western banking system froze in its tracks. Global growth collapsed and as the world prepared for a long recession, India counted its lucky stars that its financial system had escaped unscathed

rates. The average growth rate of the economy was around 4 per cent before the 1980s. It increased to an average of about 8 per cent since 2004.

But all good things must come to an end. In 2008, the global financial crisis struck. The Western banking system froze in its tracks. Global growth collapsed and as the world prepared for a long recession, India counted its lucky stars that its financial system had escaped unscathed. This ensured growth would continue even as the rest of the world stumbled from one crisis to another.

IN his budget speech of 2010-11, the Finance Minister, Pranab Mukherjee highlighted the grave uncertainties which the Indian economy had faced in 2008-09, with growth decelerating and business sentiment becoming weak. The economy's capacity to sustain high growth was under serious threat from the widespread economic slowdown in the developed world. The short term global outlook was bleak and the consensus was that year 2009 would face the brunt of this crisis across the world. At home, there was added uncertainty on account of the delayed and sub-normal south-west monsoon, which had undermined the kharif crop in the country. There were concerns about production and prices of food items and its possible repercussions on the growth of rural demand.

However, India weathered these crises well, although challenges remained, which, as Pranab Mukherjee stated would continue to engage the Indian policy-planners for the next few years. The challenges were reverting to higher growth path of 9 per cent, for which the Finance Minister sought Lord Indra's help, to harness economic growth to consolidate the recent

Growth brings in its wake infrastructure development

gains in making development more inclusive and addressing the weaknesses in government systems and institutions at different levels of governance.

The Budget of 2011-12 was presented in a much better mood, and the Finance Minister said : "Our growth in 2010-11 has been swift and broad-based. The economy is back to its pre-crisis growth trajectory. While agriculture has shown a rebound, industry is regaining its earlier momentum. Servic-

es sector continues its near double digit run. Fiscal consolidation has been impressive. This year has also seen significant progress in those critical institutional reforms that would set the pace for double-digit growth in the near future".

In some ways this budget was of a different kind. There were some statements made which made it evident that the Union Budget cannot be a mere statement of Government accounts. It has to reflect the Government's vision and signal

The outsourcing revolution resulted in the creation of a plethora of technology jobs for Indian youngsters

the policies to come in future.

It was stated that "in a complex and rapidly evolving economy, the Government cannot profess to be the sole repository of all knowledge. Indeed, in a democratic polity, it stands to benefit from inputs from colleagues on both sides of the House. They must lend their voice and expertise to influence public policy in the wider national interest". Further, the FM stated " I see the Budget for 2011-12 as a transition towards a more transparent and result oriented economic management system in India. We are taking major steps in simplifying and placing the administrative procedures concerning taxation, trade and tariffs and social transfers on electronic interface, free of discretion and bureaucratic delays. This will set the tone for a newer, vibrant and more efficient economy". Furthermore it was stated "At times the biggest reforms are not the ones that make headline, but the ones concerned with the details of governance, which affect the everyday life of aam aadmi. In preparing this year's Budget, I have been deeply conscious of this fact".

IT must be left to future historians to decide what role good policy played and how far it was the inertia of the previous six years that kept India on a high growth path, albeit with increasingly high inflation after 2007. But by the end of 2011, it had become clear that the new decade was going to be very troublesome. Prime Minister Manmohan Singh's new year message to the nation on January 1, 2012 summed up the situation with precise gloom:

"As I look ahead I see Five Key Challenges facing the nation. To meet these challenges we need the concerted efforts of the Central Government, the State Governments, political parties and indeed all concerned citizens...

"First, there is the urgent challenge of eradicating poverty, hunger and illiteracy and providing gainful employment to all. I call this the challenge of livelihood security...Along with education and affordable healthcare, we must also generate a growth process that can provide gainful employment to all... The second challenge that demands our attention is economic security. Economic security comes from having an economy that can produce the material output required to achieve desired consumption levels for the people and one that can generate the productive jobs needed to satisfy the aspirations of the workforce. To reach this level we will have to ensure rapid growth accompanied by adequate job creation. Rapid growth is also necessary to generate the revenues we need to finance our livelihood security programmes. The process of economic reforms was initiated in the mid-1980s and accelerated in the 1990s precisely to accelerate our growth potential. Because of our democratic system, the reforms were introduced gradually to begin with, in order to garner broad based support. That we succeeded in this objective is evident from the fact that successive governments of different political complexions at the centre, and many governments belonging to different political parties in the states, have more or less pushed in the same direction. However, this gradualist pace also meant that the full effects of the reforms took time to have effect. Yet, the fruits of this effort have been amply evident in the past several years. The average growth rate of the economy was around 4 per cent per year before the 1980s. It increased to an average of about

> It must be left to future historians to decide what role good policy played and whether it was the inertia of the previous six years that kept India on a high growth path, albeit with high inflation after 2007. But by the end of 2011, it had become clear that the new decade would be troublesome

Liberalisation has unleashed a consumerist culture

8 per cent since 2004...

"To achieve sustained rapid growth we need to do more than halt the current slowdown though that is certainly the first step. We need to usher in a second agricultural revolution to ensure sufficient growth in rural incomes. We also need to usher in the many reforms needed to trigger rapid industrialisation and to build the infrastructure which such industrialisation needs...Our urban population is expected to grow from 380 million at present to 600 million by 2030. We must be able to provide productive jobs in the non-agricultural sector for this expanding urban population and we must also be able to expand our urban infrastructure to deal with the expected expansion of the urban population...

"A critical element in ensuring economic security and prosperity is the need for fiscal stability. India has paid a heavy price in the past for fiscal profligacy. Many of us can recall the dark days of 1990-91 when we had to go around the world begging for aid. Fortunately we were able to overcome the problem fairly quickly and for most of the past two decades we have been able to hold our head high, because we have managed our fiscal resources well.

WE must ensure that the country does not go down that road once again...I am concerned about fiscal stability in future because our fiscal deficit has worsened in the past three years. This is mainly because we took a conscious decision to allow a larger fiscal deficit in 2009-10 in order to counter the global slowdown.

That was the right policy at the time. But like other countries that resorted to this strategy, we have run out of fiscal space and must once again begin the process of fiscal consolidation. This is important to ensure that our growth process is

The twin goals of expanding new investment and achieving energy efficiency require a more rational pricing policy, aligning India's energy prices with global prices

not jeopardised and, equally important, our national sovereignty and self-respect are not endangered...

"The most important step for restoring fiscal stability in the medium term is the Goods and Services Tax. This would modernise our indirect tax system, increase economic efficiency and also increase total revenues. Another important step is the phased reduction in subsidies. Some subsidies, such as food subsidies are justifiable on social grounds and are expected to expand once the Food Security Bill becomes operational. But there are other subsidies that are not and these must be contained...

"The third challenge we face, is the challenge of energy security. Energy is an essential for development because higher levels of production inevitably involve larger energy use. Our percapita energy levels are so low that we need, and must plan for, a substantial growth in energy availability...The domestic agenda for energy security is clear.

We need new investment in established sources of energy such as coal, oil, gas, hydro-electricity and nuclear power. We also need investment in new sources of energy, like solar and wind... Parallel with expanding domestic supplies, we need to promote energy efficiency to contain the growth of energy associated with rapid growth.

Both goals of expanding new investment and achieving energy efficiency require a more rational pricing policy, aligning India's energy prices with global prices. ...unless we achieve this transition we will not be able to promote energy efficiency as much as we should, and we will certainly not be able to attract enough investment to expand domestic energy supplies...We also need a pro-active foreign policy, protecting our access to such resources and to foreign technology..."

Speech on March 4, 1991

YASHWANT SINHA, FINANCE MINISTER

The new Government, which assumed office in mid-November 1990, inherited an economic situation of crisis proportions. The budget deficit of the Central Government reached a level of Rs 13,000 crore, on 30th November 1990,

as a consequence of revenue shortfalls and expenditure overruns. The Wholesale Price Index registered an increase of 8.5 per cent, while the Consumer Price Index rose by 11.9 per cent, during the first eight months of the current financial year.

The sharp deterioration in the balance of payments situation led to a rapid depletion of foreign exchange reserves, which dropped to Rs 3142 crore at the end of November 1990 and this sum was not even sufficient to finance imports for one month.

These developments were not an unfortunate coincidence, but were the outcome of shortcomings in the macro-management of the economy in the past. I say this neither in a spirit of acrimony nor with a desire to apportion blame. But the time has come for the Government to share its concerns with the Parliament and the people, in an endeavour to evolve a national consensus so that the restoration of the health of the economy is perceived as a collective responsibility.

Macro-economic imbalances which have been large and persistent are at the root of the problem. The fiscal deficits of the Government had to be met by borrowing at home. The current account deficits of the economy were inevitably financed by borrowing from abroad. The burden of servicing the accumulated internal and external debt has now become onerous. I need hardly stress that neither the Government nor the economy can live beyond its means for long. The room for maneuver, to live on borrowed money or time, has been used up completely. The soft options have been exhausted.

It is not surprising that the persistent fiscal imbalances have accentuated inflationary pressures in the economy and strained the balance of payments. Thus, even at the beginning of the current financial year, the economy was in a serious fiscal crisis and faced a very difficult balance of payments situation. These problems have been sharply exacerbated by the oil shock and the dislocations caused by the crisis and the war in the Gulf. We have experienced a deterioration in the fiscal situation. Consumers are faced with double digit inflation. The economy is faced with a balance of payments crisis. The impact of the Gulf war on the economy, in the year to come, is difficult to assess fully at this point of time. The level at which international oil prices would stabilise thereafter cannot be predicted.

On assumption of office, we could not have waited and allowed a further deterioration in the budgetary situation. Therefore, without losing any time, I introduced a package of measures to mobilise additional revenue. Steps were taken to improve tax compliance and revenue collections. The strictest possible control was exercised on expenditure. At the same time, I had also assured the Parliament that the Government attached a very high priority to fiscal consolidation, even if it meant hard

decisions and difficult choices which had been postponed for long. I would like to stress, once again, that my commitment to fiscal adjustment in 1991- remains firm and irrevocable.

In the difficult set of circumstances, where the uncertainties remain, we shall need some more time to evolve a comprehensive strategy for restoring the health of the economy. In formulating the Budget, we want to ensure that such a macro-economic adjustment does not disrupt the rhythm of the growth process and does not place a burden on the poor. What is more, the process of fiscal correction needs to be situated in a medium term perspective. We are engaged in the formulation of a comprehensive approach which would provide a satisfactory and sustainable solution to these problems. This needs time. I would, therefore, plead with the House to wait until the regular Budget for 1991-92 is presented in May 1991.

BUDGET SPEECH FOR 1997-98

P CHIDAMBARAM, FINANCE MINISTER

...The Government headed by Prime Minster Shri Deve Gowda completes nine months today. When I stood before this House on July 22, 1996, this House received my proposals with a mixture of wonder, curiosity and scepticism. I was, after all, the Finance Minister of the genuine coalition government at the Centre. I was also the first Finance Minister who belonged to an avowed regional party, albeit with a national outlook.

Hon'ble Members will indulge me for a few minutes while I reflect on those eventful days in May 1996. One national party acknowledged that it had lost its claim to form the government. Another tried, but failed. It is in that situation that regional parties, and certain parties with a larger national presence, came together to form the United Front Government. These parties-long regarded as children of a lesser God-have demonstrated that, given the opportunity, they can form a government not only at the State level but also at the Centre.

There is a strong continuity between my first Budget and the present one. The foundation of the Budget remains the Common Minimum Programme. The experience of the last eight months has demonstrated the enormous strengths of the programme. Drawing on the CMP, my first Budget articulated seven broad objectives. These objectives embraced vital elements such as growth, basic minimum services, employment, macroeconomic stability, investment (particularly in infrastructure), human development and a viable balance of payments. I believe these objectives remain as valid today as they were eight months ago.

...Macroeconomic management involves, inevitably, striking a balance between various objectives and considerations. As Hon'ble Members are aware, in 1995-96, the growth in money supply was reduced sharply to 13.2 per cent. Although this helped to contain inflation, it also led to high real interest rates, a widespread perception of a liquidity crunch and a slackening of investment proposals. Since July 1996, corrective action has been taken which has eased the availability of money and brought down the interest rates. The long-delayed increase in the prices of petroleum products and supply-side problems, arising mainly out of lower production and lower procurement of wheat in the last season, exerted pressure on the price level. Government has taken a number of steps to maintain price stability.

Paddy production and procurement in the Kharif season have been satisfactory and we have adequate stocks of rice. The Rabi wheat crop is also very promising and steps will be taken to maximise procurement. At the same time, I would like to make it clear that, if necessary, government will not hesitate to import wheat and other essential articles to counter the pressure on prices. Maintaining price stability is high on the agenda of this Government... Our goal is to break inflationary expectations and reduce the rate of inflation from the present level....

Hon'ble Members will recall that in my last Budget speech I had promised to present concrete proposals in this Budget to phase out the system of ad hoc treasury bills by 1997-98. I am glad to announce that the government and the RBI have worked out the specific measures in this regard.

54 . The system of ad hoc treasury bills to finance the budget deficit will be discontinued with effect from April 1, 1997. A scheme of ways and means advances (WMA) by the RBI to the Central Government is being introduced to accommodate temporary mismatches in the government's receipts and payments. This will not be a permanent source of financing the government's deficit. Besides ways and means advances, RBI's support will be available for the government's borrowings programme. Details of the scheme are being separately announced by the RBI.

55 . What I am effecting today is a bold and radical change which will strengthen fiscal discipline and provide greater autonomy to RBI in the conduct of the monetary policy. With the discontinuance of ad hoc treasury bills and tap treasury bills, and the introduction of ways and means advances, the concept of Budget deficit, as currently defined, will lose its relevance either as an indicator of short term requirement of funds by the government or the extent of monetisation.

Therefore, it is proposed to discontinue the practice of showing the 'Budget deficit'; instead Gross Fiscal Deficit (GFD) would become the key indicator of deficit. The extent of RBI support to the Central government's borrowing programme will be shown as "monetised deficit" in the Budget documents.

...What will we do without our critics? As Saint Tiruvalluvar said: "Idipparai Illatha Emara Mannan Keduppar Ilanum Kedum" (Behold the King who reposeth not on those who can rebuke him/ He will perish even when he hath no enemies.)

... I have decided to lower the rates of personal income-tax across-the-board in a significant manner. The current rates of 15, 30 and 40 per cent are being replaced by the new rates of 10, 20 and 30 per cent.

...Turning to corporate taxes, I had in my last budget reduced the rate of surcharge from 15 per cent to 7.5 per cent and had expressed the hope that I would take a similar step in my next

Union Finance Minister P Chidambaram arriving at Parliament House for the Budget 2008-09

budget. I propose to abolish the balance surcharge on companies...Corporates should be encouraged to undertake new investments. Hence, I propose to reduce the tax rate applicable to both domestic and foreign companies. The rate for domestic companies will now be 35 per cent and for foreign companies 48 per cent...

The Minimum Alternate Tax (MAT) on companies, which was introduced last year, has been the subject of extensive debate. A large number of representations have been received to repeal—or review—the provisions. The economic rationale for MAT has, I am afraid, not been altered and I am unable to accept the request that the provision introduced last year be totally withdrawn. However, there is a case for a review of the manner in which the tax is charged and collected...

Now, I turn to my indirect tax proposals... On more than one occasion, I have stated that we would achieve the average levels of tariffs prevalent in ASEAN countries by the turn of the century...This year's proposals should be seen in this background.

I propose to reduce the peak rate of customs duty from 50 per cent to 40 per cent...

I have introduced three new rates, namely, 8 per cent 13 per cent and 18 per cent. In the process I have done away with the rates of 20 per cent and 10 per cent (except in the case of some petroleum products).

In the interest of revenue, I have perforce to continue, for the time being, the rate of 15 per cent which will apply to metals and a few other commodities...I hope to bring the fiscal deficit under 4 per cent in the next budget.

...Other Asian countries are surging ahead. China is powering its way to becoming the second largest economy in the world. These countries have shown that with courage, wisdom and pragmatism they can find their rightful places in the world.

[28th February, 1997]

Budget Speech 1991-92

MANMOHAN SINGH,

FINANCE MINISTER

24th July, 1991

PART A

"Sir,

I rise to present the budget for 1991-92. As I rise, I am overpowered by a strange feeling of loneliness. I miss a handsome, smiling, face listening intently to the Budget Speech. Shri Rajiv Gandhi is no more. But his dream lives on; his dream of ushering India into the twenty-first century; his dream of a strong, united, technologically sophisticated but humane India. I dedicate this budget to his inspiring memory.

2. The new Government, which assumed office barely a month ago, inherited an economy in deep crisis. The balance of payments situation is precarious. International confidence in our economy was strong until November 1989 when our Party was in office. However, due to the combined impact of political instability witnessed thereafter, the accentuation of fiscal imbalances and the Gulf crisis, there was a great weakening of international confidence. There has been a sharp decline in capital inflows through commercial borrowing and non-resident deposits.

As a result, despite large borrowings from the International Monetary Fund in July 1990 and January 1991, there was a sharp reduction in our foreign exchange reserves. We have been at the edge of a precipice since December 1990 and more so since April 1991. The foreign exchange crisis constitutes a serious threat to the sustainability of growth processes and orderly implementation of our development programmes. Due to the combination of unfavourable internal and external factors, the inflationary pressures on the price level have increased very

Union Finance Minister Manmohan Singh arriving in the Parliament House to present the Budget for 1993-94

substantially since mid-1990. The people of India have to face double digit inflation which hurts most the poorer sections of our society. In sum, the crisis in the economy is both acute and deep. We have not experienced anything similar in the history of independent India.

3. The origins of the problem are directly traceable to large and persistent macro-economic imbalances and the low productivity of investment, in particular the poor rates of return on past investments. There has been an unsustainable increase in Government expenditure. Budgetary subsidies, with questionable social and economic impact, have been allowed to grow to an alarming extent. The tax system still has many loopholes. It lacks transparency so that it is not easy to assess the social and economic impact of various concessions built into its structure. The public sector has not been managed in a manner so as to generate large investible surpluses. The excessive and often indiscriminate protection provided to industry has weakened the incentive to develop a vibrant export sector. It has also accentuated disparities in income and wealth. It has worked to the disadvantage of the rural economy. The increasing difference between the income and expenditure of the Government has led to a widening of the gap between the income and expenditure of the economy as a whole. This is reflected in growing current account deficits in the balance of payments.

4. The crisis of the fiscal system is a cause for serious concern. The fiscal deficit of the Central Government, which measures the difference between revenue receipts and total expenditure, is estimated at more than 8 per cent of GDP in 1990-91, as compared with 6 per cent at the beginning of the 1980s and 4 per cent in the mid-1970s. This fiscal deficit had to be met by borrowing. As a result, internal public debt of the Central Government has accumulated to about 55 per cent of Gross Domestic Product (GDP). The burden of servicing this debt has now become onerous. Interest payments alone are about 4 per cent of GDP and constitute almost 20 per cent of the total expenditure of the Central Government. Without de-

cisive action now, the situation will move beyond the possibility of corrective action.

5. The balance of payments situation is most difficult. The current account deficit, which was about 2 per cent of GDP for several years, is estimated to be more than 2.5 per cent of GDP in 1990-91. These persistent deficits, which were inevitably financed by borrowings from abroad, have led to a continuous increase in external debt which, including non-resident Indian (NRI) deposits, is estimated at 23 per cent of GDP at the end of 1990-91. Consequently, the debt service burden is estimated at about 21 per cent of current account receipts in 1990-91. These strains were stretched to a breaking point on account of the Gulf crisis last year. The balance of payments has lurched from one liquidity crisis to another since December 1990. The current level of foreign exchange reserves, in the range of Rs 2500 crore, would suffice to finance imports for a mere fortnight.

6. The price situation, which is of immediate concern to the vast mass of our people, poses a serious

There is no time to lose. Neither the Government nor the economy can live beyond its means year after year. The room for maneuver, to live on borrowed money or time, does not exist any more. Any further postponement of macroeconomic adjustment, long overdue, would mean that the balance of payments situation, now exceedingly difficult, would become unmanageable and inflation, already high, would exceed limits of tolerance.

problem as inflation has reached a double digit level. During the fiscal year ending 31st March 1991 the wholesale price index registered an increase of 12.1 per cent, while the consumer price index registered an increase of 13.6 per cent. The major worrisome feature of the inflation in 1990-91 was that it was concentrated in essential commodities. The prices of these commodities rose inspite of the three good monsoons in a row and hence the three successive bumper harvests. Inflation hurts everybody, more so the poorer segments of our population whose incomes are not indexed.

7. There is no time to lose. Neither the Government nor the economy can live beyond its means year after year. The room for maneuver, to live on borrowed money or time, does not exist any more. Any further postponement of macroeconomic adjustment, long overdue, would mean that the balance of payments situation, now exceedingly difficult, would become unmanageable and inflation, already high, would exceed limits of tolerance. For improving the management of the economy, the starting point, and indeed the centre-piece of our strategy, should be a credible fiscal adjustment and macro-economic stabilisation during the current financial year, to be followed by continued fiscal consolidation thereafter. This process would, inevitably, need at least three years, if not longer, to complete. But there can be no adjustment without pain. The people must be prepared to make necessary sacrifices to preserve our economic independence and restore the health of our economy.

8. In the macro-management of the economy, over the medium-term, it should be our objective to progressively reduce the fiscal deficit of the Central Government, to move towards a significant reduction of the revenue deficit, and to reduce the current account deficit in the balance of payments. It is only such prudent management that would enable us to curb the exponential growth in internal and external debt and limit the burden on debt servicing, for the Government and the country, to manageable levels. Indeed, we must make a conscious effort to reduce the internal debt of

the Government and the external debt of the nation, so that we rely more and more on our own resources to finance the process of development.

During the period of transition, it shall be our endeavour to minimise the burden of adjustment on the poor. We are committed to adjustment with a human face. It will also be our endeavour that the adjustment process does not adversely affect the underlying growth impulses in our economy. We do not have time to postpone adjustment and stabilisation. We must act fast and act boldly. If we do not introduce the needed correctives, the existing situation can only retard growth, induce recession and fuel inflation, which would hurt the economy further and impose a far greater burden on the poor.

9. Macro-economic stabilisation and fiscal adjustment alone cannot suffice. They must be supported by essential reforms in economic policy and economic management, as an integral part of the adjustment process, reforms which would help to eliminate waste and inefficiency and impart a new element of dynamism to growth processes in our economy. The thrust of the reform process would be to increase the efficiency and international competitiveness of industrial production, to utilise for this purpose foreign investment and foreign technology to a much greater degree than we have done in the past, to increase the productivity of investment, to ensure that India's financial sector is rapidly modernised, and to improve the performance of the public sector, so that the key sectors of our economy are enabled to attain an adequate technological and competitive edge in a fast changing global economy. I am confident that, after a successful implementation of stabilisation measures and the essential structural and policy reforms, our economy would return to a path of a high sustained growth with reasonable price stability and greater social equity. Barriers to entry and limits on growth in the size of firms, have often led to a proliferation of licensing and an increase in the degree of monopoly. This has put shackles on segments of Indian industry and made them serve the interests of producers but not pay adequate attention to the interests of con-

sumers. There has been inadequate emphasis on reduction of costs, upgradation of technology and improvement of quality standards. It is essential to increase the degree of competition between firms in the domestic market so that there are adequate incentives for raising productivity, improving efficiency and reducing costs. In the pursuit of this objective, we have announced important changes in industrial policy which will bring about a significant measure of deregulation in the domestic sector, consistent with our social objectives and the binding constraints on the balance of payments. The policies for industrial development are intimately related to policies for trade.

There can be no doubt that protection was essential in the initial phase of our industrial development, so that we could go through the learning period without disruption. The past four decades have witnessed import substitution which has not always been efficient and has some times been indiscriminate. The time has come to expose Indian industry

The thrust of the reform process would be to increase the efficiency and international competitiveness of industrial production, to utilise for this purpose foreign investment and foreign technology to a much greater degree, to increase the productivity of investment, to ensure that India's financial sector is modernised, and to improve the performance of the public sector, so that the key sectors of our economy attain an adequate technological and competitive edge in a fast changing global economy

to competition from abroad in a phased manner. As a first step in this direction, the Government has introduced changes in import export policy, aimed at a reduction of import licensing, vigorous export promotion and optimal import compression.

The exchange rate adjustments on 1st and 3rd July 1991 and the enlargement and liberalisation of the replenishment licence system constitute the two major initial steps in the direction of trade policy reform. They represent the beginning of a transition from a regime of quantitative restrictions to a price based mechanism. After four decades of planning for industrialisation, we have now reached a stage of development where we should welcome, rather than fear, foreign investment. Our entrepreneurs are second to none.

Our industry has come of age. Direct foreign investment would provide access to capital, technology and markets. It would expose our industrial sector to competition from abroad in a phased manner. Cost, efficiency, and quality would begin to receive the attention they deserve. We have, therefore, decided to liberalise the policy regime for direct foreign investment in the following manner. First, direct foreign investment in specified high priority industries, with a raised limit for foreign equity at 51 per cent, would be given prompt approval, if equity inflows are sufficient to finance the import of capital goods at the stage of investment and if dividends are balanced by export earnings over a period of time. Second, foreign equity upto 51 per cent would be allowed for trading companies primarily engaged in export activities. Third, a special board would be constituted to negotiate with a number of large international firms and approve direct foreign investment in selected areas; this would be a special regime to attract substantial investment that would provide access to high technology and to world markets.

Our banking system and financial institutions are at the very core of the financial infrastructure in the economy. The widening and deepening of our financial system have helped the spread of in-

The Finance Minister of Pakistan Mehbub-ul-Haq (centre) with the then Deputy Chairman of Planning Commission Manmohan Singh on his left and Minister of State for Planning Ajit Panja in New Delhi on November 15, 1985

stitutional finance over a vast area and have contributed significantly to the augmentation of our savings rate, particularly financial savings. This has been a most commendable achievement, but our financial system has developed certain rigidities and some weaknesses which we must address now. The objective of reform in the financial sector would be to preserve its basic role as an essential adjunct to economic growth and competitive efficiency, while improving the health of its institutions. In this task, it is essential to ensure capital adequacy, introduce prudential norms and improve profitability of our commercial banks and financial in-

stitutions. There are no magic solutions. These are complex issues which need careful consideration. Therefore, I propose to appoint a high-level committee to consider all relevant aspects of structure, organisation, functions and procedures of the financial system. This Committee would advise the Government on appropriate measures that would be needed to enhance the viability and health of our financial sector so that it can better serve the needs of the economy without any sacrifice of the canons and principles of a sound financial system. As we enter the last decade of the twentieth century, India stands at the cross-roads. The decisions

we take and do not take, at this juncture, will determine the shape of things to come for quite some time. It should come as no surprise, therefore, that an intense debate rages throughout the country as to the path we should adopt. In a democratic society it could not be otherwise.

What can we learn from this debate? The most important thing that comes out clearly is that we cannot realise our goal of establishing a just society, if we abandon the planning process. But India's future development depends crucially on how well the planning process is adapted to the needs of a fast changing situation. I believe that

Growing urbanisation requires planning processes that are sensitive to the needs of a dynamic economy

without an intelligent and systematic coordinated resource use in some major sectors of our economy, development will be lopsided. It will violate deeply cherished values of equity and it will keep India well below its social, intellectual and moral potential. But our planning processes must be sensitive to the needs of a dynamic economy. Over centralisation and excessive bureaucratisation of economic processes have proved to be counter productive.

We need to expand the scope and the area for the operation of market forces. A reformed price system can be a superior instrument of resource allocation than quantitative controls. But markets can only serve those who are part of the market system. A vast number of people in our country live on the edges of a subsistence economy. We need credible programmes of direct government intervention focussing on the needs of these people. We have the responsibility to provide them with quality social services such as education, health, safe drinking water and roads. In the same way,

the development of capital and technology intensive sectors, characterised by long gestation periods, such as transport and communications and energy will need to be planned with much greater care than ever before. The control of land and water degradation, which threatens the livelihood of millions of poor people in this country, will also require effective Government leadership and action.

The challenge that we are facing is without precedent. In its initial stages, the Industrial Revolution in the western world concentrated on the creation of wealth, unmindful of the social misery and inequity which characterised this process. The democratisation of the polity came much later. The socialist experiment in charting a new path for accelerated industrial transformation of an underdeveloped economy and polity did achieve considerable success in developing technological and military capabilities, accumulation of capital for rapid industrial growth and human resources development, in countries such as the USSR. But recent developments have shown that this approach too suffered from major weaknesses, particularly in its allocative efficiency, in the management of technical change, control of environmental degradation and in harnessing the vast latent energy and talents of individuals. In India, we launched an experiment under the leadership of Pandit Jawaharlal Nehru, an experiment which sought to unite the strengths and merits of different approaches to accelerated development of our backward economy.

We have achieved considerable success in the field of development, modernisation and greater social equity. However, we are yet far from realising our full potential in all these areas. We have to accomplish the unfinished task, while remaining steadfast in our allegiance to the values of a democratic system. At the same time, we must restore to the creation of wealth its proper In highlighting the significance of reform, my purpose is not to give a fillip to mindless and heartless consumerism we have borrowed from the affluent societies of the West. My objection to the consumerist phenomenon is two-fold. First, we cannot afford it. In a society where we lack drinking water, education, health, shelter and other basic necessities, it would be tragic if our productive resources were to be devoted largely to the satisfaction of the needs of a small minority. The country's needs for water, for drinking and for irrigation, rural roads, good urban infrastructure, and massive investments in primary education and basic health services for the poor are so great as to effectively preclude encouragement to

> The country's needs for water, for drinking and for irrigation, rural roads, good urban infrastructure, and massive investments in primary education and basic health services for the poor are so great as to effectively preclude encouragement to consumerist behaviour imitative of advanced industrial societies. Our approach to development has to combine efficiency with austerity. Austerity not in the sense of negation of life or a dry, arid creed that casts a baleful eye on joy and laughter

consumerist behaviour imitative of advanced industrial societies. Our approach to development has to combine efficiency with austerity. Austerity not in the sense of negation of life or a dry, arid creed that casts a baleful eye on joy and laughter. To my mind, austerity is a way of holding our society together in pursuit of the noble goal of banishing poverty, hunger and disease from this ancient land of ours. Before I conclude, let me end on a personal note. Years ago, in a letter which Jawaharlal Nehru wrote to the young Indira Gandhi, he advised her that in dealing with the affairs of the State one should be full of sentiment but never be sentimental. But the House will forgive me if on an occasion like this I cannot avoid being somewhat sentimental.

151. I was born in a poor family in a chronically drought prone village which is now part of Pakistan. University scholarships and grants made it possible for me to go to college in India as well as in England. This country has honoured me by appointing me to some of the most important public

offices of our sovereign Republic. This is a debt which I can never be able to fully repay. The best I can do is to pledge myself to serve our country with utmost sincerity and dedication. This I promise to the House. A Finance Minister has to be hard headed. This I shall endeavour to be. I shall be firm when it comes to defending the interests of this nation. But I promise that in dealing with the people of India I shall be soft hearted. I shall not in any way renege on our nation's firm and irrevocable commitment to the pursuit of equity and social justice. I shall never forget that ultimately all economic processes are meant to serve the interests of our people. It is only through a commitment to social justice and the pursuit of excellence that we can mobilise the collective will of our people for development, to give it a high moral purpose and to keep alive the spirit of national solidarity. The massive social and economic reforms needed to remove the scourge of poverty, ignorance and disease can succeed only if backed by a spirit of high idealism, self sacrifice and dedication.

152. The grave economic crisis now facing our country requires determined action on the part of Government. We are fully prepared for that role.

Our party will provide an effective Government to our country. Our people are our masters. We see the role of our Government as one of empowering our people to realise their full potential. This budget constitutes a vital component of a comprehensive vision, a well thought out strategy and an effective action programme designed to get India moving once again.

153. Sir, I do not minimise the difficulties that lie ahead on the long and arduous journey on which we have embarked. But as Victor Hugo once said, "no power on earth can stop an idea whose time has come." I suggest to this august House that the emergence of India as a major economic power in the world happens to be one such idea. Let the whole world hear it loud and clear. India is now wide awake. We shall prevail. We shall overcome.

[24th July, 1991]

Speech on February 28, 2011

PRANAB MUKHERJEE, FINANCE MINISTER

We are reaching the end of a remarkable fiscal year. In a globalised world with its share of uncertainties and rapid changes, this year brought us some opportunities and many challenges as we moved ahead with steady steps on the chosen path of fiscal consolidation and high economic growth.

2. Our growth in 2010-11 has been swift and broad-based. The economy is back to its pre-crisis growth trajectory. While agriculture has shown a rebound, industry is regaining its earlier momentum. Services sector continues its near double digit run. Fiscal consolidation has been impressive. This year has also seen significant progress in those critical institutional reforms that would set the pace for double-digit growth in the near future.

3. While we succeeded in making good progress in addressing many areas of our concern, we could have done better in some others. The total food inflation declined from 20.2 per cent in February 2010 to less than half at 9.3 per cent in January 2011, but it still remains a concern. In the medium term perspective, our three priorities of sustaining a high growth trajectory; making development more inclusive; and improving

our institutions, public delivery and governance practices, remain relevant. These would continue to engage the Indian policy-planners for some time. However, there are some manifestations of these challenges that need urgent attention in the short term.

4. Though we have regained the pre-crisis growth momentum, there is a need to effect adjustments in the composition of growth on demand and supply side. We have to ensure that along with private consumption, the revival in private investment is sustained and matches pre-crisis growth rates at the earliest. This requires a stronger fiscal consolidation to enlarge the resource space for private enterprise and addressing some policy constraints. We also have to improve the supply response of agriculture to the expanding

Pranab Mukherjee leaving North Block for Parliament to present the 2011-12 Budget

domestic demand. Determined measures on both these issues will help address the structural concerns on inflation management. It will also ensure a more stable macroeconomic environment for continued high growth.

5. The UPA Government has significantly scaled up the flow of resources to rural areas to give a more inclusive thrust to the development process. The impact is visible in the new dynamism of our rural economy. It has helped India navigate itself rapidly out of the quagmire of global economic slowdown. Yet, there is much that still needs to be done, especially in rural India. We have to reconcile legitimate environmental concerns with necessary developmental needs. Above all, there is the 'challenge of growing aspiration' of a young India.

6. To address these concerns, I do not foresee resources being a major constraint, at least not in the medium-term. However, the implementation gaps, leakages from public programmes and the quality of our outcomes are a serious challenge.

7. Certain events in the past few months may have created an impression of drift in governance and a gap in public accountability. Even as the Government is engaged in addressing specific concerns emanating from some of these events in the larger public interest and in upholding the rule of law, such an impression is misplaced. We have to seize in these developments, the opportunity to improve our regulatory standards and administrative practices. Corruption is a problem that we have to fight collectively.

8. In a complex and rapidly evolving economy, the Government can not profess to be the sole repository of all knowledge. Indeed, in a democratic polity, it stands to benefit from inputs from colleagues on both sides of the House. They must lend their voice and expertise to influence public policy in the wider national interest. In some areas, good results depend on coordinated efforts of the Centre and the State Governments and in some others, on favourable external developments.

9. I see the Budget for 2011-12 as a transition towards a more transparent and result oriented economic management system in India. We are taking major steps in simplifying and placing the administrative procedures concerning taxation, trade and tariffs and social transfers on electronic interface, free of discretion and bureaucratic delays. This will set the tone for a newer, vibrant and more efficient economy.

10. At times the biggest reforms are not the ones that make headline, but the ones concerned with the details of governance, which affect the everyday life of aam aadmi. In preparing this year's Budget, I have been deeply conscious of this fact.

12. Our principal concern this year has been the continued high food prices. Inflation surfaced in two distinct episodes. At the beginning of the year, food inflation was high for some cereals, sugar and pulses. Towards the second half, while prices of these items moderated and even recorded negative rates of inflation, there was spurt in prices of onion, milk, poultry and some vegetables.

FINANCIAL SECTOR LEGISLATIVE INITIATIVES

34. The financial sector reforms initiated during the early 1990s have borne good results for the Indian economy. The UPA Government is committed to take this process further. Accordingly, I propose to move the following legislations in the financial sector:

(i) The Insurance Laws (Amendment) Bill, 2008;

(ii) The Life Insurance Corporation (Amendment) Bill, 2009;

(iii) The revised Pension Fund Regulatory and Development Authority Bill, first introduced in 2005;

(iv) Banking Laws Amendment Bill, 2011;

(v) Bill on Factoring and Assignment of Receivables;

(vi) The State Bank of India (Subsidiary Banks Laws) Amendment Bill, 2009; and

(vii) Bill to amend RDBFI Act 1993 and SARFAESI Act 2002.

35. In my last Budget speech, I had announced that Reserve Bank of India would consider giving some additional banking licences to private sector players. Accordingly, RBI issued a discussion paper in August, 2010, inviting feedback from the public. RBI has proposed some amendments in the Banking Regulation Act. I propose to bring suitable legislative amendments in this regard in this session. RBI is planning to issue the guidelines for banking licences before the close of this financial year.

FINANCIAL SECTOR LEGISLATIVE REFORMS COMMISSION

48. In pursuance of the announcement made in Budget 2010-11, the Government has set up a Financial Sector Legislative Reforms Commission under the Chair of Justice B. N. Srikrishna. It would rewrite and streamline the financial sector laws, rules and regulations and bring them in harmony with the requirements of a modern financial sector. The Commission will complete its work in 24 months.

CORRUPTION

128. A Group of Ministers has been constituted to consider measures for tackling corruption. The Group has been tasked with addressing issues relating to State funding of elections, speedier processing of corruption cases of public servants, transparency in public procurement and contracts, discretionary powers of Central ministers and competitive system for exploiting natural resources. The Group will make its recommendations in a time bound manner.

Indian financial history at a glance

Current Account Deficit/GDP

1.7

-1

GDP at Factor Cost

2.3

54.9

3.04

25.2

GDP at Factor Cost

Gross Fiscal Deficit/GDP

Current Account Deficit/GDP

WPI Headline

FE Reserves
(USD Million)

Population below Poverty Line

Foodgrain Production
(Million Tonnes)

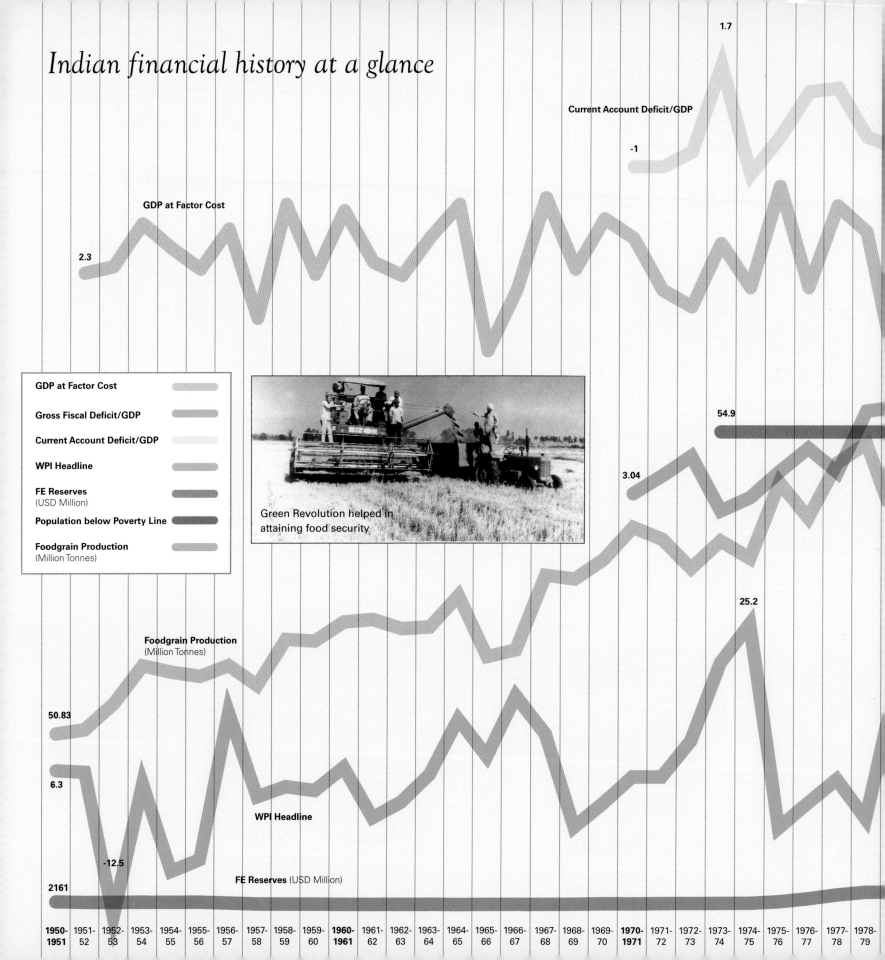

Green Revolution helped in
attaining food security

Foodgrain Production
(Million Tonnes)

50.83

6.3

WPI Headline

-12.5

FE Reserves (USD Million)

2161

| **1950-**
1951 | 1951-
52 | 1952-
53 | 1953-
54 | 1954-
55 | 1955-
56 | 1956-
57 | 1957-
58 | 1958-
59 | 1959-
60 | **1960-**
1961 | 1961-
62 | 1962-
63 | 1963-
64 | 1964-
65 | 1965-
66 | 1966-
67 | 1967-
68 | 1968-
69 | 1969-
70 | **1970-**
1971 | 1971-
72 | 1972-
73 | 1973-
74 | 1974-
75 | 1975-
76 | 1976-
77 | 1977-
78 | 1978-
79 |

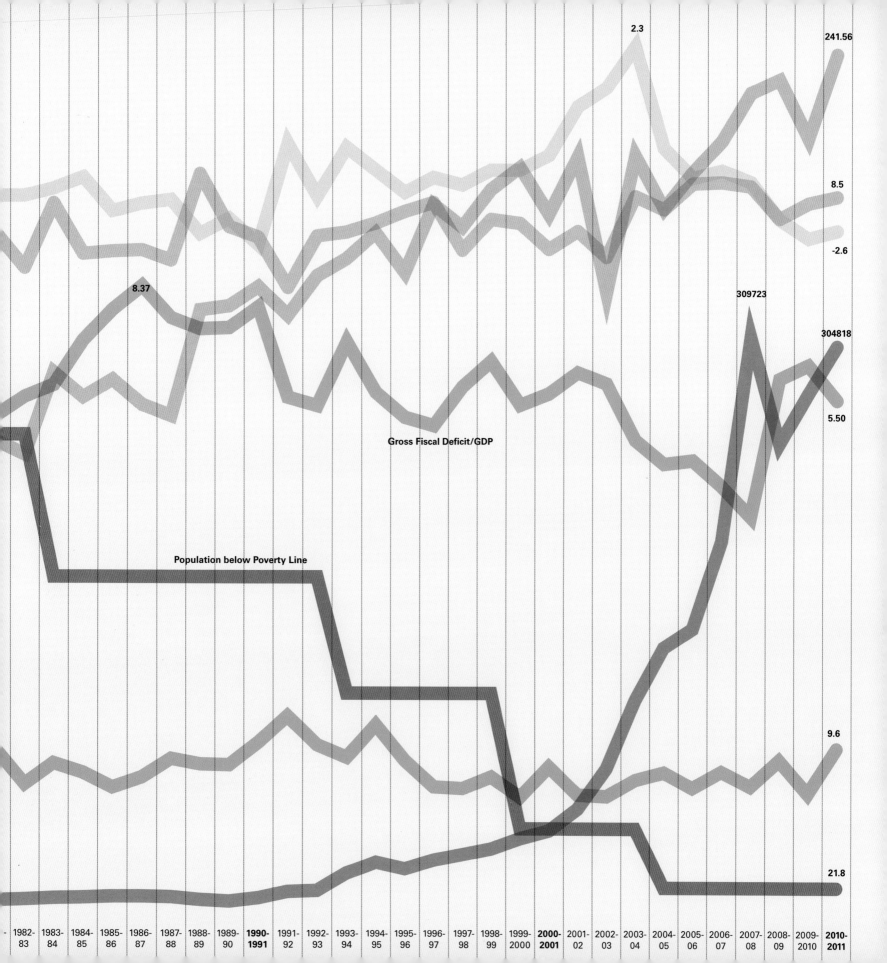

2.3

241.56

8.5

-2.6

8.37

309723

304818

5.50

Gross Fiscal Deficit/GDP

Population below Poverty Line

9.6

21.8

1982-
83
1983-
84
1984-
85
1985-
86
1986-
87
1987-
88
1988-
89
1989-
90
**1990-
1991**
1991-
92
1992-
93
1993-
94
1994-
95
1995-
96
1996-
97
1997-
98
1998-
99
1999-
2000
**2000-
2001**
2001-
02
2002-
03
2003-
04
2004-
05
2005-
06
2006-
07
2007-
08
2008-
09
2009-
2010
**2010-
2011**

Index

A

Authority 28, 29, 30, 32, 64, 97

B

Balance of payments 19, 49, 51, 57, 61, 72, 73, 49, 79, 87, 88, 90, 91
Borrowing 37, 38, 40, 41, 74, 87, 88, 90, 91
Budget speech 38, 61, 73, 80, 88, 90, 97
Bureaucracy 51, 59, 68

C

Cabinet 26, 27, 28, 29, 30, 32, 33, 79
  Cabinet Secretariat 26, 29
Capital Goods 52, 72, 92
CEA 17, 19
  Chief Economic Advisor 5, 9
Chaudhury, Sachin 57
Chetty, R.K. Shanmukham 37, 38, 41
Chidambaram, P 79, 88
Committee 23, 26, 28, 29, 30, 31, 32, 33, 39, 47, 93
  Estimates Committee 39
Communists 79
Congress 45, 46, 49, 61, 62
  Avadi Congress 45
  Congress Party 57, 59, 79
Constitution 27, 30, 39, 61
Credit 41, 46, 53, 53, 68, 46

D

Debt 68, 73, 74, 91, 95
  External debt 87, 91, 92
  Internal debt 74, 91
Desai, Morarji 46, 57, 59, 61, 62
Desai, Nitin 20
Deshmukh, Chintamani 39, 40, 45
Devaluation 47, 47
Drought 51, 57, 68, 74, 95

E

Economic growth 10, 80, 93, 96

Economist 9, 10, 20, 26, 29, 30, 31, 32, 40, 41, 47, 62
EFF 73
Emergency 61
Energy security 86
Expenditure 37, 41, 45, 52, 59, 61, 74, 79, 87, 91
Exports 29, 52, 57, 62, 68, 72, 74
Extended Fund Facility 73

F

Finance Minister 12, 15, 20, 29, 37, 39, 44, 45, 46, 53, 57, 59, 61, 62, 72, 68, 79, 80, 81, 88, 90, 95
Finance Ministry 20, 37, 39, 45, 46, 49, 57, 62, 74
Fiscal Deficit 40, 57, 79, 86, 87, 88, 89, 91
Fiscal Policy 80
Five Year Plan 40, 45, 46, 68

G

Gandhi, Indira 47, 51, 56, 57, 59, 61, 62, 64, 65, 68, 72, 75, 95
Gandhi, Mohandas Karamchand
  Mahatma 2, 41
Gandhi, Rajiv 72, 74, 79, 90
Gandhi, Sanjay 61
GDP 38, 57, 68, 72, 79, 91
Government 9, 10, 19, 20, 28, 30, 31, 32, 33, 37, 38, 39, 40, 41, 47, 48, 57, 59, 61, 62, 68, 72, 73, 74, 75, 79, 80, 81, 85, 87, 88, 90, 91, 92, 93, 94, 95, 97
  Government of India 9, 28, 48, 53

I

IAS 29
  Indian Administrative Service 20
IES 9, 10, 19, 20
  Indian Economic Service 9, 10, 20
IMF 19, 68, 72, 73
  International Monetary Fund 90
Imports 29, 38, 39, 52, 57, 68, 72, 74, 79, 87, 91
income tax 45, 61, 64, 68, 75, 79

Income Tax 46
Independent 31, 37, 46, 79, 91
Industrial licensing 61, 72, 79
Industrial Policy 45, 92
Inflation 19, 38, 39, 41, 57, 61, 68, 74, 85, 87, 88, 90, 91, 92, 96, 97
Infrastructure 72, 86, 88, 92, 95
Investment 38, 40, 46, 49, 52, 53, 57, 59, 60, 64, 68, 72, 49, 79, 86, 88, 89, 91, 92, 95

J

Jagjivan Ram, Babu 27
Jain, Ajit Prasad 27
Jalan, Bimal 17, 80
Janata party 61

K

Krishnamachari, T.T. 27, 39, 44, 45, 52
  TTK 45, 46, 49, 57
Krishnamachari, V.T. 26, 29, 32
Krishna Menon, V.K. 27

L

Lahiri, Ashok K. 19
Liberalisation 20, 62, 79, 92

M

Mahalanobis, P.C. 27, 29, 30, 32
Mathai, John 38, 39, 40, 62
Ministry of Home Affairs 27, 28, 29, 30, 32, 33
Monetary policy 80, 88
Mukherjee, Pranab 14, 72, 73, 80

N

Nanda, Gulzarilal 27
Nehru, B.K. 39
Nehru, Jawahar Lal 10, 18, 25, 27, 38, 39, 40, 45, 46, 49, 57, 59, 61, 95

P

Pant, Govind Ballabh 27

ARTWORKS AND PHOTOGRAPHS BY

Cover: Anil Ahuja

Page 2: Gandhi Smriti Archives

Page 3, 5, 9, 36-37, 40, 82-83, 98-99: Anil Ahuja

Page 10: Kaushik Basu

Page 21, 38, 39, 41, 51, 58, 65, 75, 87, 89: The Hindu Archives

Page 11, 23, 35, 43, 55, 67, 77: Puja Ahuja

Page 81: Arvind Yadav/Hindustan Times (courtesy Academic Foundation)

Page 84: courtesy Academic Foundation
top: Ajay Agarwal/Hindustan Times
bottom-left: Manpreet Singh
bottom-right: Rituraj Kapila

Page 94: Sudhir Kumar (courtesy Academic Foundation)

All other photographs, courtesy: Photo Division, Ministry of Information and Broadcasting, Government of India